SECRET CHICAGO

A GUIDE TO THE WEIRD, WONDERFUL, AND OBSCURE

Jessica Mlinaric

Reedy Press
PO Box 5131
St. Louis, MO 63139
www.reedypress.com

Library of Congress Control Number: 2017958844
ISBN: 9781681060705

Design by Jill Halpin

Printed in the United States of America
21 22 5 4 3

For Joe, Chris, Christina, and Steve Mlinaric, who taught me that every place holds adventure worth exploring.

"And then when I went to Chicago, that's when I had these outer space experiences and went to the other planets."
—Sun Ra

"There is not a day that passes that I do not find my head filled with images from Chicago's history."
—Rick Kogan

CONTENTS

INTRODUCTION

How did a grave end up in a scrapyard? What Chicago building has a connection to ancient Egypt? Did the first nuclear reactor ever *leave* Chicago? Why does the West Loop smell like brownies? For every question I answer about Chicago, three more spring up.

I had plenty of questions when I moved to Chicago nearly a decade ago. Many of these ideas even stumped Chicago natives! So I started my own cultural explorations of this strange, alluring, and, at times, intimidating city.

This book is a guide for people who want to see a hidden side of Chicago. It's for Chicagoans eager to step beyond their neighborhood boundaries and visitors looking for experiences they won't find anywhere else.

Secret Chicago highlights unknown locations all over the city. From the corners of Beverly and Rogers Park to the heights of the Loop. Some sites bring you face to face with Chicago's mysterious past. Others are present-day places that offer a different perspective on this fantastic city.

Whole worlds are lost inside Chicago's buildings and around street corners. To dig them up, I consulted community groups, historical societies, journalists, tour guides, bartenders, strangers at breakfast, fellow photographers in the festival photo pits, and longtime locals across the city.

There's no way to discover all Chicago's secrets, but this book is a starting point for your extraordinary adventures. Don't be selfish—please reveal your *Secret Chicago* explorations on social media using #SecretChicago! Let's uncover Chicago's stories together.

ACKNOWLEDGMENTS

Bringing Chicago's history to life takes a team. I'm particularly grateful to the following people for their insight and encouragement.

Thanks to Wendy Bright, Scott Cramer, Jeff Danna, Abhijeet Rane, Rod Sellers, Z. J. Tong, and everyone else who took the time to share their community with me. Thank you, Kathleen Dragan, Casey Forquer, Matt Gambatese, Max Grinnell, Mark Guarino, Aaron Lorence, Nick Nummerdor, Chuck Sudo, Dakota Sillyman, Jon Shaft, and Phillip Solomonson for your helpful suggestions.

To the Chicago Public Library, the Chicago History Museum, and Janet Harper at the Center for Black Music Research at Columbia College Chicago.

Thanks to Zac Bleicher, Richard Bley, Virginia Carstarphen, Christen Carter, Joel Carter, Allison Dincecco, Natalie Edwards, Greg Fischer, Patrick Hatton, Margaret Hicks, Tim Horsburgh, Jacquelyn Jenke, Janine Judge, Pete Knefel, Sandra Lachler, Peter Mars, Eve Rodriguez Montoya, Luke Nevin-Gattle, Rocko Onan, Tyler Stoltenberg, Shayna Swanson, Maya Jahmil Wallace, and Jesse Zavala for your time and hospitality.

Jim Bachor, Jojo Baby, Thomas Kong, Gordon Quinn, and Gavin Rayna Russom: thank you for sharing your story with me. I'm honored to include your work.

Thanks to Kelly O'Donnell and Megan Lehnert, who provided early feedback and editorial suggestions. Thank you, Christina Mlinaric, for providing scientific research assistance. Ladies, sharing your wisdom and encouragement meant more than you know.

Molly Page, thank you for believing in me and for your insight and support throughout this process. Chicago is lucky to have you. To the team at Reedy Press, thank you for helping turn all these hours of research into a real book, my first!

Thank you to Blake Levinson and J. J. McDowell, who knew I was writing this book long before I did.

Thanks to my blog readers at urbnexplorer.com and my editors at *Chicagoist* for first giving me a place to share Chicago's stories.

To my family and friends, I couldn't have done this without you. Thank you for your encouragement, patience, and enthusiasm. Thanks to those who trekked all over Chicago with me—under city streets, into silos, and beyond.

Brett Hayes, I can't begin to thank you for all your support throughout this process. There is no one I'd rather explore Chicago, or life, with.

1 PRESIDENTIAL KISS AND TELL

Why is this shopping center a destination for lovebirds?

This Hyde Park shopping center might not look like much, but it's the site of a romantic presidential monument. A historic plaque marks the spot where a young Barack Obama shared a first kiss with his future wife, Michelle.

In 1989, Obama landed a summer job as an associate at the Chicago law firm where Michelle worked. After several requests for a date, Michelle finally agreed to go out with the smitten future president. According to a 2007 interview with *O, The Oprah Magazine*, Obama sealed the date with a kiss.

"On our first date, I treated her to the finest ice cream Baskin-Robbins had to offer, our dinner table doubling as the curb. I kissed her, and it tasted like chocolate."

A plaque commemorates this quote at the location of the first couple's budding romance. Under a photo of the pair embracing, it reads, "On this site, President Barack Obama first kissed Michelle Obama."

Get the twenty-four-dollar "Obama cut" at the Hyde Park Hair Salon next to the shopping center. The "official barbershop of President Obama" has even preserved his favorite chair in a plexiglass display case.

This marker commemorates the sweet start of a historic relationship. The Obamas' first date also included a visit to the Art Institute, a stroll down Michigan Avenue, and a screening of Spike Lee's film Do the Right Thing.

OBAMA FIRST KISS PLAQUE

WHAT Site of the first couple's first kiss

WHERE S. Dorchester Ave. and E. 53rd St.

COST A Baskin-Robbins scoop will set you back $2.79

PRO TIP Pick up a chocolate ice cream cone at the Dorchester Commons Baskin-Robbins like Michelle Obama did.

The plaque is mounted on a three-thousand-pound granite boulder and surrounded by a modest garden. The owners of the Dorchester Commons shopping center commissioned the plaque as a marker for community, posterity, and tourism.

Baskin-Robbins has moved a few doors down, but amorous visitors can still grab a scoop in the neighborhood and reenact this famous first smooch.

2 THE OTHER SEARS TOWER

Is there more than one Sears Tower in Chicago?

The term "Sears Tower" suggests an architectural icon and engineering triumph that was the world's tallest building for twenty-four years. Yet before that landmark was built and later renamed the Willis Tower, Chicago had *another* Sears Tower.

In 1906 Sears, Roebuck & Company built a headquarters in North Lawndale befitting its title as the world's largest mail-order company. The forty-one-acre complex contained a plant that printed the famous Sears catalog, its own power plant, and a three-million-square-foot mail-order plant. Boasting nine thousand employees and forty thousand orders mailed daily, it was the largest commercial building in the world at the time.

Attached to the Merchandise Building was a fourteen-story warehouse structure known as the Sears Tower. It housed offices, training facilities, an observation deck, and a 200,000-gallon water tank for the fire sprinkler system. The tower even broadcasted WLS-AM radio from the eleventh floor. The call letters are a reference to the station owner, "World's Largest Store."

When Sears moved its headquarters to the new Sears Tower downtown in 1974, the complex sadly lost its luster.

At one time, the Sears complex contained athletic courts, a sunken garden, and an automotive center. The first Sears retail store opened here in 1925, and it included an optical shop and a soda fountain.

Top, *Wave to the second Sears Tower and the rest of the skyline from the fourteenth-floor event space.* Bottom, *The original Sears Tower stands 250 feet high, compared to its 1,450-foot sibling downtown.*

NICHOLS TOWER

WHAT A historic skyscraper

WHERE 906 S. Homan Ave.

COST Free

PRO TIP Look for the Sears, Roebuck & Company initials on the restored staircase.

Much of the site was demolished in the 1990s, but the tower remained in a state of vacant decay.

Thankfully, this wasn't the last stand for the original Sears Tower. It's now listed on the National Register of Historic Places, and the surrounding area has developed into an affordable housing community called Homan Square.

In 2016, a $15 million renovation of the tower was completed. This Sears Tower was also renamed. It's now the John D. and Alexandra C. Nichols Tower in honor of its benefactors. It serves as a community center and event space with tenants that include education, arts, and media nonprofits. The restored observatory boasts 360-degree views of Chicago and the revitalizing North Lawndale neighborhood.

CREATIVE CONVENIENCE

Where can I find a convenience store that doubles as an art gallery?

In the city's northernmost neighborhood, Rogers Park, the search for public art becomes a scavenger hunt on viaducts, underpasses, and sea walls. One resident displays art in an even more unlikely location—his corner store.

The Mile of Murals project seeks to paint a full mile of murals along the CTA Red Line track between Estes Avenue and Pratt Boulevard. The project has installed fourteen thousand square feet of artwork since 2007. Artists apply for one or two new mural tracts each year and have come from around the country to contribute.

Installed in 2017, *Be Happy* took its inspiration from a nearby convenience store. The mural was designed by Thomas Kong, who owns Kim's Corner Food. Kong's cut-out art installations displayed in the store's window are a neighborhood favorite.

The mural can't prepare you for stepping into the dizzying delight of the store. Kong's minimal collages cover the walls, shelves, coolers, even the merchandise. They are bright, optimistic, and witty. Kong has created more than ten thousand collages, working every day for the past seven years.

Kong creates his work using surplus material from the store, like product labels and cardboard boxes. Between serving customers, he uses scissors to cut organic shapes from a juice label or pack of gum. Familiar faces like the

KIM'S CORNER FOOD

WHAT Art in aisle one

WHERE 1371 W. Estes Ave.

COST Free

PRO TIP View a mural map and guide at mileofmurals.com.

Left, *"I just glue things that look good to me with the materials that happen to be around me,"* says Kong. Right, *The collages in Kong's store inspired Roman Susan Art Foundation to collaborate with him on an eighty-foot mural. Look for it on the railway embankment on Glenwood Avenue at Estes Avenue.*

Keebler elf appear next to abstract forms. Tucked in the back of the store is an archive and exhibit space called the Back Room. The space features installations of Kong's art curated by other artists.

Although Kong started making the collages to decorate the store, he has a new mission. "Now it is to give people happiness for the rest of my life," Kong said in an interview with Jisu Lee. "That's why the catchphrase is 'Be Happy.' It is a command." It only takes a few moments in Kong's whimsical world to oblige.

Elsewhere in Rogers Park, repurposed metal and toys find new life as art at the Glenwood Avenue Sculpture Garden. Another tradition is painting the Loyola Beach sea bench each summer at the Artists of the Wall Festival.

4 KNOCKIN' ON HEAVEN'S DOOR

Where can I get closer to heaven?

Humans are always trying to reach the heavens. It's not hard to do in Chicago, where you can send your prayers upward from the world's tallest church.

The First United Methodist Church at the Chicago Temple was founded in 1831 before Chicago was even a city! The city's oldest church first met in a log cabin, built in 1834. A few years later, they floated it across the Chicago River and rolled it on logs to the corner of Washington and Clark Streets. The church has called this prime piece of real estate home ever since.

The current structure was the tallest building in town when it was built in 1924. The city even raised the building height limit to accommodate the Gothic skyscraper. On the first floor, a sanctuary seats five hundred worshipers. The space features a wood altar carving of Jesus weeping over Jerusalem as well as stained glass windows depicting the Old and New Testaments. Other floors include chapels,

The church's 150th anniversary celebration in 1981 included two choirs, a forty-four-piece band, and costumes representative of the 1830s. Mayor Jane Byrne led the procession in a horse-drawn carriage from the church to its original location across the river.

Take a tiny elevator or 173 steps to arrive at the Sky Chapel. Stained glass windows illuminate scenes from the Bible, the history of the Methodist Church, and the congregation's history. This panel depicts the present-day church.

FIRST UNITED METHODIST CHURCH OF CHICAGO

WHAT World's tallest church

WHERE 77 W. Washington St.

COST Free tours are offered Monday through Saturday at 2 p.m. and on Sunday after each worship service.

NOTEWORTHY The sixth floor of the building once held the office of Clarence Darrow, the famous trial attorney.

offices, a nursery, the parsonage, and a small museum. Several floors are rented out to lawyers who value the building's location in the heart of the Loop.

Those who really want to get close to the Big Guy in the Sky can take two elevators and a set of stairs to the Sky Chapel. The chapel is tucked inside the old bell tower on the twenty-seventh floor. It was a gift from the Walgreen family in 1952 in memory of store founder Charles Walgreen. A companion to the altar downstairs, this one depicts Jesus weeping over Chicago.

There is a qualification to the church's claim as tallest in the world. At 568 feet tall, the mixed-use building's Sky Chapel is considered the highest place of worship above street level. The tallest building devoted entirely to religious purposes is Germany's 530-foot-tall Ulm Minster. Even so, the views up here will make anyone a believer.

5 FLYING HIGH

Can I run away to the circus in a Logan Square church?

A former evangelical church in Logan Square was built in 1908 to get closer to heaven, but its newest congregation finds different ways to soar. These days, the building's colorful stained glass windows are the backdrop for feats of flight by acrobatic, trapeze, and aerial silk artists. Career and recreational circus enthusiasts learn how to fly through the air with the greatest of ease at Aloft Circus Arts.

Shayna Swanson founded Aloft in 2005 to embody "the innovation of the new circus movement, the daring of the traditional big top shows, and the joy and comedy of vaudeville." Aloft purchased the church in 2016, finding its expansive floor space and high ceilings to be an ideal fit for their unique needs. After removing the pews, plaster walls, and tin ceiling, rigging was installed up to forty feet high, and the six-thousand-square-foot space was converted into six training spaces. The church balcony is now a tramp wall, used for bouncing off a trampoline and running off the wall. Even the church's bell tower was converted for circus training.

Aloft offers a full-time, two-year training program for those looking to join or start a small circus. For the circus-curious, Aloft offers a ten-dollar "taster" class to introduce different disciplines in one ninety-minute session.

Some neighbors still visit looking for church services. According to Swanson, "We're not ready to blow our cover."

ALOFT CIRCUS ARTS

WHAT Where you can still run away and join the circus

WHERE 3324 W. Wrightwood Ave.

COST Drop-in classes, $28; ticket to monthly performance, $25

PRO TIP Aloft produces a public performance on the first Saturday of every month.

"Adults don't have enough opportunities for play," says Swanson. "The circus offers a joyous release that people don't really do otherwise."

Billed as the country's third-largest circus school, Aloft saw its student enrollment double after moving to Logan Square. Acrobats of all skill levels and ages are welcome at Aloft to learn "the steps towards making gravity irrelevant." Classes include instruction in trapeze, aerial silks, tightwire, pole acrobatics, trampoline, hand balancing, and clowning.

The historic church still inspires wonder by watching high-flying students defy physics in a dramatic setting. It's good to know that the next time you have the urge to run away and join the circus, you won't have to go far.

6 REST IN PIECES

Is a soldier's grave hidden in a South Side scrapyard?

A scrapyard on Chicago's Southeast Side isn't what you would call a peaceful resting place. Between the industrial setting and rusting machinery, it's the last place you'd want to spend eternity. Yet burial here was one man's last wish, and it's still honored today.

Andreas von Zirngibl's story started far from Chicago. He was born in Bavaria in 1797 and joined the Prussian army at age eighteen. He even helped defeat Napoleon at the Battle of Waterloo, where he lost an arm. Afterward, Andreas started a family and began a career as a fisherman.

In 1854, von Zirngibl moved to the small town of Chicago with his wife and five children. He bought forty acres of land along the Calumet River for $160 in gold. He settled there and resumed the fishing trade on Lake Michigan. Just a year after arriving in Chicago, von Zirngibl died of a fever.

According to legend, his last wish was to be buried on his homestead. His family marked the grave with a wooden cross and built a white picket fence around his grave. Although they moved to the North Side, they continued to visit over the years.

Decades later, the Calumet and Chicago Canal and Dock Company acquired the land. Andreas's relatives disputed ownership in the Illinois Supreme Court. The family claimed

---

GRAVE OF ANDREAS VON ZIRNGIBL

WHAT Chicago's smallest cemetery

WHERE 9331 S. Ewing Ave.

COST Free

PRO TIP The gravesite is located on private property. Call Sims Metal Management or the Southeast Chicago Historical Society to arrange a visit.

The neighborhood sure has changed since Andreas von Zirngibl settled here in 1854.

their property deed was lost in the Great Chicago Fire, but the company claimed von Zirngibl was a squatter. The court ruled that the company owned the land but that the grave must remain intact no matter, and the family was granted permanent access to the gravesite.

Industry grew up around the former homestead. Today, concrete blocks mark the grave where a wooden cross once did. At about one hundred square feet, it may be the city's smallest cemetery, but its caretakers over the years have honored von Zirngibl's last wish.

Writer Mike Royko recounted the battle of industrialization vs. immigrants for the von Zirngibl land in a 1967 article in the *Chicago Daily News*.

GOOD VIBRATIONS

Is Fulton Market home to a creative vortex?

Before it was home to Chicago's trendiest restaurants, Fulton Market earned a reputation as an enclave for warehouse parties and creative types. Those in the know attribute the abundance of creative talent to something more than natural skills—a vortex.

What is a vortex? According to Mars Gallery, it's a "center of creative energy that many people feel vibrate through their bodies and minds." People and animals are drawn to vortices, where energy exists on multiple dimensions and interacts with one's inner self.

Vortex locations are usually reserved for Earth's mystical natural sites like Sedona and are rarely found in urban settings. However, Mars Gallery was reportedly located over one of these "energy vortex circles" during its 30-year tenure at this location.

"When I'm all by myself, I can almost feel a low frequency," says artist and gallery owner Peter Mars. "Whatever is going on seems to stimulate creativity. A lot of the artists have commented on it."

FULTON MARKET VORTEX

WHAT The secret to Chicago's creativity

WHERE 1139 W. Fulton Market

COST Free

PRO TIP Visitors are welcome to leave tokens of thanks at the center of the vortex. Please do not move them, as some consider this sacred ground.

This battered sign leads the way to Chicago's creative wellspring.

But don't take Peter's word for it. In 2002, the *Chicago Journal* hired a shaman to inspect the vortex. Parapsychologist Naba Lamoussa examined the gallery with a walking stick, tapping the floor and walls. His findings confirmed an energy vortex near the back of the building.

If you're interested in tapping into this well of creative energy, head to the alley near the building's rear loading docks. You'll know you've reached the epicenter when you see spray paint on the street and a collection of tokens that artists and other visitors leave to thank the vortex. Whether or not you feel a rush of creativity after visiting the vortex, you're bound to get inspired by the many art galleries and creative spaces nearby.

A vortex is a good place for artists, according to Lamoussa. "The kind of energy you see here has an effect on the brain," he said.

8 COVERT COCKTAILS

Is a Lakeview B&B hiding a speakeasy in its basement?

To much of the world, Chicago is still known as the home of Al Capone's crime outfit and Prohibition-era speakeasies. Scarface may be long gone, but the city's penchant for hidden watering holes remains. You never know where you might find one, including a nondescript alleyway next to a Lakeview bed and breakfast.

The Old Chicago Inn, a B&B located in a 1906 greystone, has a secret. Its basement isn't harboring old boxes—instead it's home to a private 1920s-themed speakeasy named Room 13. The bar stays true to its Jazz Age inspiration from the décor to the cocktails.

Bartenders serve classic American cocktails using only alcohol brands that were available during Prohibition, so kiss beer and vodka goodbye in favor of whiskey, gin, and champagne concoctions. All ingredients are freshly made.

While you sip, the bartender will regale you with the history and cultural significance of your cocktail. On Saturdays, the neon-lit room may be bouncing with live music. Settle into an oversized vintage armchair and admire the room's décor, trimmed with items from the era. From the phonograph to the working rotary pay phone, you'll be Lindy hopping and toasting the giggle water in no time!

The bar's name is a play on an old superstition. Many hotels avoid naming rooms with the unlucky number "13" in them. The basement is also the 13th "room" in the building.

You won't find moonshine in this thirty-three-seat speakeasy, just handcrafted sidecars, Corpse Revivers, and other Jazz Age cocktails.

True to the speakeasy spirit, they don't let just anyone in at Room 13. To find the discreet entrance, look for the alley gate next to the B&B sporting a "RM-13" sign. If the red light is on, drinks are being poured. Knock on the door and you'll be asked for the password. *Password?* Yep, admission to Room 13 is reserved for members and hotel guests given access to the ever-changing password. Decades after the end of Prohibition, Chicagoans still appreciate an intimate drinking setting, but we're grateful that speakeasies have upgraded from bathtub gin!

THE OLD CHICAGO INN

WHAT History served straight up

WHERE 3222 N. Sheffield Ave.

COST Cocktails start at $9. Order a "Speakeasy Flight" of four historic cocktail samples plus bar snacks for $55 per couple.

PRO TIP Room 13 opens at 6 p.m. on Thursday, Friday, and Saturday nights.

9 WARRIORS WITHOUT WEAPONS

Why are these two statues empty-handed?

Grant Park is fortunate to have two imposing sentinels standing guard at its entrance, but they won't be much use in the event of an attack. That's because *The Bowman* and *The Spearman* are lacking their respective weapons.

The striking bronze sculptures of Native Americans on horseback are the work of Croatian sculptor Ivan Meštrović. The silhouettes of these majestic warriors, which stand thirty-five feet high atop granite pedestals, have framed Congress Plaza since 1928. The statues' muscular, Art Deco figures are poised for battle, but their hulking hands are empty. So where are the bow and spear?

Some people believe the weapons were stolen by pranksters. Another theory attributes the removal of the weapons to a symbolic show of respect after the attacks of September 11, 2001.

In reality, the weapons never existed. According to a 2008 *Chicago Tribune* article, Meštrović included a real bow and spear in his first sketches and models of the sculptures. He removed them to emphasize the beauty of the human body over the tools of war. The weapons are left to the imagination as the viewer focuses on the strongly defined features of the figures and their horses in motion.

Daniel Burnham's original plan for the area included one Native American sculpture and one "Buffalo Bill–like" statue.

French sculptor Auguste Rodin once said that Meštrović was "the greatest phenomenon among sculptors" and "greater than I am."

Commemorating Native Americans and the struggle of America's expansion, this powerful pair calls viewers not to conflict but to reflection. Visitors can picture the sculptural subjects thundering across Chicago's prairie past while standing among its modern skyscrapers.

THE BOWMAN AND THE SPEARMAN

WHAT Statues that seem to be missing something

WHERE Congress Pkwy. at Michigan Ave.

COST Free

NOTEWORTHY The statues inspired a Chicago punk rock band to take the name Bow & Spear.

DUSTY HUNTING

Where can I dig for obscure soul LPs in a West Side basement?

Chicago is a vinyl lover's paradise. Boasting a storied musical legacy and record shops all over the city, it's a crate-digging destination for music devotees from all over the world. Those who are serious about hunting for lost treasure head to West Garfield Park.

Out of the Past Records is the result of forty years of collecting and selling vinyl. Owners Marie and Charlie Henderson have crammed two buildings floor to ceiling with overstock records, cassettes, CDs, DVDs, and eight-track tapes. They estimate that the store contains over a million records.

The store's vast inventory is overwhelming. Most LPs aren't organized, so you never know what you'll find flipping through the stacks. Out of the Past specializes in blues, soul, R&B, gospel, and jazz from the 1960s through the '80s. Your patience may be rewarded when an overlooked corner contains boxes of sealed Smokey Robinson records, straight from the manufacturer, or old-school house mixtapes.

The basement also contains heaps of unopened cassettes and records. Vinyl fanatics fly from the United

---

The Hendersons lost their first store in the 1968 riots that ravaged the neighborhood after Dr. Martin Luther King's death. They keep a copy of the April 7, 1968, Chicago Sun-Times near the front of the store to remind patrons of the events.

Out of the Past is home to over a million records and a cross-eyed store cat named Shadow.

Kingdom, Japan, and more to put on gloves and a mask and spend days digging for gold in the basement. Collectors have even asked to be locked in the store overnight to continue their quest after hours.

"We have a large selection of older wax we bought when the record companies were just dumping LPs," Charlie Henderson told *AustinTalks*. "In the '80s, we were buying them by the box."

The Hendersons have watched the music industry and their neighborhood shift since moving there in 1963. Their collection once spanned ten shops around the city, but today they own two stores on Madison Avenue. Out of the Past Records opened in 1986. This crowded, dusty shop is a neighborhood meeting place, an international music destination, and a great place for music lovers to get schooled.

GREEN MACHINE

What Chicago brewery will be powered by food waste?

Chicago's Back of the Yards neighborhood has a legacy of food production. For decades, the nearby Union Stock Yard was the nation's meat-packing powerhouse, as grimly noted in Upton Sinclair's The Jungle. Meat magnate Gustavus Swift even bragged that his facilities were so efficient they used "everything but the squeal." These days, one facility is putting a sustainable spin on that concept of economy.

A hulking former 93,500 square foot pork processing plant has found new life as The Plant. Established in 2011 by Bubbly Dynamics, The Plant is a vertical farm that aims to reimagine waste. By connecting small food businesses under one roof, founder John Edel's ultimate mission is to create collaborative communities focused on material reuse and energy conservation.

THE PLANT

WHAT A vertical farm victory

WHERE 1400 W. 46th St.

COST Tour tickets cost $10 or $7 for students and seniors; free for Back of the Yards residents

PRO TIP Buy food direct from the source at The Plant's retail shop, the Turtle Stop, or during farmers markets.

The Plant is home to twenty sustainable small food businesses. Nothing goes to waste in this collaborative community. Carbon dioxide from Whiner Beer Co.'s brewing system is used as an input to processes in indoor farms and algae bioreactors. Whiner Beer Co. also salvaged waste honeycombs from urban beekeepers Bike a Bee and added it to a batch of sour ale for a honey-infused collaboration called Save the Queen. Bubbly Dynamics repurposed a 9,000-gallon tank formerly used by Peer Foods to hold brine for pickling pork products as a cistern to collect rooftop runoff. This allows

Top, *The Plant is also home to the Packingtown Museum, which hosts lectures, film screenings, and educational programs on the history of the Union Stock Yard and Chicago's industrial future.* Bottom, *Whiner Beer Co. focuses on barrel-aged beer, a tradition common in Belgium and France. Whiner aims to promote environmentally responsible brewing, and their spent grain will help fuel The Plant's anaerobic digester.*

growers to use commercial drip tape and walking irrigation systems, increasing crop yields and saving on tap water bills.

Eventually, The Plant will be powered by biogas emitted from an anaerobic digester. The enormous metal tank will convert thirty tons of food waste a day from resident businesses and other community partners. The digester will provide process heat for its processes and fuel boilers, chillers, roasters, and more. It will demonstrate that even food-production businesses, which are typically waste and energy intensive, can operate sustainably by closing waste loops.

The Plant hosts a variety of events including tours, markets, and workshops. The former meatpacking facility even offers vegan markets! Fifty years after the closing of the stockyards, Back of the Yards is back at the forefront of food production.

Using an anaerobic digester, The Plant hopes to eventually divert more than ten thousand tons of food waste from landfills each year. That's enough electricity to power more than 250 homes.

12 THAT TODDLIN' TOWN

Why are vintage beer ads immortalized on some Chicago buildings?

At first glance, a painted globe carved into a building's facade might just seem like pretty ornamentation. Look closer and you'll notice this is actually an advertisement for Schlitz beer. What are these ads and why are they all over Chicago?

It turns out that these buildings are former tied houses. These were pre-Prohibition saloons owned or subsidized by breweries that in turn sold beer exclusively from that brewery. According to a 2010 report by the city of Chicago, the city was home to a whopping seven thousand saloons in 1893, and half of them were tied to breweries. About forty-one tied-house buildings survive today.

Tied houses were built by big breweries like Schlitz and Pabst as well as local players like Peter Hand and Stege. Often located near rail lines or industrial complexes, they catered to Chicago's working class. Tied houses were constructed with an appealing architectural style to convey an air of decency and civic pride, in opposition to the depictions of saloons by the growing temperance movement as vice dens. Tied houses are typically found in Chicago's neighborhoods at the corners of two commercial streets. They feature a trademark of their sponsoring brewery, usually a logo depicted in stone, metal, or glass.

Schlitz tied houses are the most common in Chicago and are identified by the belted globe logo. It was designed for Schlitz's exhibit at the 1893 World's Columbian Exposition.

When the former tied house faced Prohibition, Southport Lanes installed bowling lanes as a speakeasy front. The vintage lanes remain and so does the practice of setting pins by hand.

TIED HOUSES

WHAT Chicago's hard-drinking past preserved

WHERE Various

COST Don't pay more than $5 for an Old Style.

PRO TIP Look for tied houses at the corners of commercial streets in Chicago's neighborhoods.

The tied-house system had many unintended consequences. It increased competition, leading some saloon keepers to allow unsavory activity on the premises and engage in kickbacks to police and officials. Resistance to these elements was one factor that eventually led to Prohibition. These days, a three-tier system regulates the sale of alcohol between producers, wholesalers, and retailers.

Today, many remaining tied houses have resumed their original role as bars. Is it economic luck that has preserved these buildings, or are bar owners the best stewards of Chicago's two-fisted past?

13 BUTTON UP

Are 1,500 pinback buttons on display inside a Logan Square business?

"I like Ike." "I Love New York." We've all seen buttons supporting political and other causes. The tiny billboards are so commonplace that their messages are often overlooked. However, one button vendor has created a museum dedicated to preserving the social history of the modest button.

Since 1995, the Busy Beaver Button Co. has been manufacturing and selling custom pinback buttons. But there's a surprise inside its Logan Square storefront. Busy Beaver is also the home of the world's only dedicated button museum.

Sibling owners Christen and Joel Carter began the museum in 2010 to showcase their growing collection of buttons. The twenty-thousand-button collection represents categories including band names, social causes, and the ever-popular smiley face buttons. The impressive range of styles on display spans mechanical buttons, litho buttons printed straight on metal, metamorphic buttons with duplicate images, Crystoglas buttons with embossed metal, and more.

Harold Washington's campaign holds the record for most mayoral campaign buttons used in an election. Hundreds of these buttons are on display in the Harold Washington exhibit at the DuSable Museum of African American History.

Busy Beaver can make about sixteen thousand buttons in a single day. They have created around thirty-seven million buttons to date. Busy Beaver is also home to the "world's largest button."

BUSY BEAVER BUTTON MUSEUM

WHAT The world's only dedicated button museum

WHERE 3407 W. Armitage Ave.

COST Free

NOTEWORTHY The 1,500 buttons on display represent only 7 percent of the total collection, which continues to grow.

The button collection tells a social story of pop culture, from the pro- and anti-Prohibition buttons of the 1920s to punk band propaganda. Their oldest button is a 1789 souvenir button marking George Washington's inauguration. Busy Beaver created glow-in-the-dark buttons for President Obama's 2008 victory rally, and they even own an 1864 Lincoln re-election campaign button.

It's incredible how much history is packed into the colorful messages of the seemingly simple button. Although one button asks, "Don't you feel stupid wasting all your time reading buttons?" the correct answer is, not anymore.

14 'TIL THE COWS COME HOME

Where can you lead a cow to pasture in the Loop?

Chicago is rampant with secret tunnels supposedly used as Prohibition-era getaway routes. One hidden passageway was built for even earlier Chicago residents, and they weren't human.

Before Chicago officially became a city in 1833, a farmer named Willard Jones purchased a ninety-foot-wide plot of land at Clark and Monroe Streets. The savvy investor sold half the land a decade later, with one provision. Jones reserved the right to continue using the ten-foot-wide cow path on the property to lead his bovine buddies to the pasture near today's Board of Trade building.

When Jones sold the remainder of this plot two years later, the deed included access to Monroe Street through the cow path. By the 1870s, transporting livestock in the Loop was illegal except for the Monroe Street cattle path.

In 1927, nearly one hundred years after Jones purchased the land, the owners of the first plot wanted to build an office building on the property. The courts granted them the right to erect a twenty-two-story building, but only if it included access to the corridor. The building's architect incorporated an eighteen-foot-high tunnel to accommodate any passing wagons or farm animals.

Chicago had a cow over the passageway in 1932. It was used for the first time

LOOP CATTLE PATH

WHAT "Out to pasture" preserved

WHERE 100 W. Monroe St.

COST Free

NOTEWORTHY One of the hotel's conference rooms is named for Willard Jones, originator of the cow path.

It's mostly used for storage these days, but this Loop corridor must remain accessible to any passing cattle.

in decades during a publicity stunt for the International Livestock Expo. A cow named Northwood Susan VI and her calf Buttercup were led through the passage with great fanfare. Chicago mayor Ed Kelly even proclaimed the corridor was "reserved forever as a cow path."

Hyatt converted the 100 West Monroe Building into a hotel, preserving the cow path. You can see the service door next to the main entrance of the Hyatt Centric Hotel. Today, the corridor is used for hotel and kitchen storage, but you can still use it as a shortcut to LaSalle street. No cattle included.

In 1969, the First National Bank of Chicago constructed a new building blocking the northern end of the cow path and diverting traffic into an alley. Both Chicago Title & Trust and the Chicago Historical Society declared that the action was legal.

15 IT'S A HIGHWAY TO HEAVEN

Was gospel music born in Chicago?

Chicago is a historic hub of blues and jazz music. Although these musical styles originated in the South, they were cultivated in Chicago after the Great Migration in the early twentieth century. Yet one of the world's most popular music genres *was* born in Chicago. The groundbreaking sounds of gospel music first rose on the city's South Side.

A music steeped in praise and hope had its roots in tragedy. Thomas A. Dorsey started his music career as a blues pianist touring with the likes of Ma Rainey in the 1920s. While on tour, his wife and infant son died in childbirth. Dorsey channeled his despair into music, writing "Take My Hand, Precious Lord" just a month later.

This new style of music incorporated blues elements like lamenting vocals and syncopated rhythms into music of faith. "I borrowed the moans, trills, and turns from blues and jazz, smoothed it out, changed the words of course, and I had gospel," Dorsey told the *Chicago Tribune* in 1978. Dorsey devoted his life to creating religious music and is

---

Thomas A. Dorsey founded the National Convention of Gospel Choirs and Choruses and the first gospel music publishing company. He wrote more than five hundred songs and was the first African American inducted into Nashville's Songwriters Hall of Fame.

EBENEZER BAPTIST CHURCH

WHAT The birthplace of gospel music

WHERE 4501 S. Vincennes Ave.

COST Free

PRO TIP Catch the Chicago Gospel Music Festival every summer. It's been running since 1985.

Built in 1899, Ebenezer Baptist Church is the last building designed by famed architect and acoustic design expert Dankmar Adler. Originally built as a synagogue, the auditorium holds 1,200 worshipers. Its barrel-vaulted auditorium and horseshoe-shaped balcony are the perfect setting for joyous songs of praise.

known as the Father of Gospel Music. The piano where he wrote that first gospel song is on display at the Chicago History Museum.

Dorsey and director Theodore Frye founded the first known gospel choir at Ebenezer Missionary Baptist Church in 1931. He trained early gospel singers including Mahalia Jackson, Roberta Martin, and Clara Ward. As gospel music spread on the South Side, these catchy songs were simply known as "Dorseys." He organized the second gospel choir in Chicago in 1932 at Pilgrim Baptist Church, where he remained the director for sixty years.

Gospel's passionate form of praise has spread around the world since its beginnings in Bronzeville, and it's easy to hear why. As Dorsey told the *Tribune*, "*Gospel* means 'good news,' and I wanted people to shout out their happy feelings, pat their feet, and clap their hands."

EYE TO THE SKY

What's that round building at Roosevelt and Halsted?

Unless you stop to inspect it, you might assume that the round, rust-colored structure standing at Roosevelt and Halsted is a squat water tower or a flying saucer on stilts. It turns out that this is an installation by a world-renowned artist, and there's more to it than meets the eye.

For starters, it's meant to be viewed from the inside. The structure, known as a "skyspace," arrived in 2006 as an observatory to view the interaction of sky, atmosphere, and light. Perceptual artist James Turrell has been building skyspaces around the world for more than forty years.

Enter the twenty-six-foot-tall structure from one of four openings and take a seat on a concrete bench. The skyspace's white ceiling and walls provide a calming interior sanctuary, while waterfalls soften outside street noise. Colored lights are set into the decorative pavement at your feet. Above, a halo of frosted glass filters in outside light.

A slice of sky is visible through a ten-by-sixteen-foot elliptical hole in the roof. This oculus frames the shifting light levels and sky. By obscuring the horizon, the "celestial vault" creates the illusion that the sky is a design on the flat ceiling. The most dramatic times to view the skyscape are

The university is built on the site of Maxwell Street Market. The shopping district drew Chicago's immigrant communities and sold virtually anything for more than one hundred years. A new iteration of the market keeps the spirit of Maxwell Street alive today.

James Turrell's skyspaces are "chambers with an aperture in the ceiling open to the sky." The artist has installed more than eighty skyspaces around the world.

SKYSPACE

WHAT An artful look up

WHERE 803 W. Roosevelt Rd.

COST Free and open every day of the year

PRO TIP The skyspace is best viewed at sunrise or sunset.

at dawn or dusk, when the sky's changing light plays off the chamber's colored lights.

Chicago's skyspace is Turrell's first to be fully public and accessible at any time. It anchors the Earl L. Neal Plaza gateway to the University of Illinois at Chicago's South Campus. Seeing the sky as though it's in reach adds a sense of wonder to the everyday. According to Turrell, his work "deals with light itself, not as the bearer of revelation, but as revelation itself." Surrounded by the hectic cityscape, the skyspace invites visitors to see Chicago in a new light.

FORGOTTEN TERMINAL 4

Why is Terminal 4 missing at O'Hare International Airport?

O'Hare is one of the world's busiest airports, and there is plenty of signage posted to guide you to your final destination. As travelers rush to their gates, few notice a mystery in plain sight. Airport signs prominently identify Terminals 1, 2, 3, and 5. So where is Terminal 4?

Terminal 4 did exist once upon a time, from 1985 to 1993. International traffic at O'Hare was picking up during the mid-1980s, and United Airlines needed more space. The airport shuffled things up. United moved into the old international hub at Terminal 1, and Terminal 4 took over international flights.

The main floor of a parking garage was converted to serve as the international terminal at what was then the world's busiest airport. It wasn't long before international airlines found it to be too small, and planning began for an even grander international terminal. The shiny new Terminal 5 opened in 1993, and temporary Terminal 4 was quietly closed.

O'Hare removed all traces of the old terminal to avoid confusing travelers accustomed to visiting Terminal 4 at

O'Hare's airport code, ORD, comes from its origin as an aircraft assembly plant called Orchard Field. It was renamed in 1949 to honor World War II aviator Edward O'Hare, but the code never changed.

Top, *Looking for Terminal 4? Then you're at the wrong airport. It was unceremoniously closed in 1993.* Bottom, *This elevator bank leads to the former site of Terminal 4.*

O'HARE INTERNATIONAL AIRPORT

WHAT A terminal that vanished into thin air

WHERE 10000 W. O'Hare Ave.

COST The elevator is located before security, so you won't need a boarding pass, just $5 for up to two hours of parking or $2.25 for a ride on the CTA Blue Line.

NOTEWORTHY ORD was the world's busiest airport for decades. It's currently the sixth busiest.

a certain location. The new international terminal received a new number. Yet there is one hint to the forgotten terminal that's still visible. Visitors may see a sign labeling Elevator Center 4. This leads to a bus and shuttle terminal located on the site of the former Terminal 4.

Terminal 4's international service may have been short-lived, but as long as the mystery of its whereabouts still puzzles observant travelers, it's not forgotten.

GOING NUCLEAR

Are the remnants of the world's first nuclear reaction buried in a Chicago forest preserve?

One of Chicago's most critical contributions to science occurred in an unusual place—a squash court under the University of Chicago's football field. On December 2, 1942, it was the site of the world's first nuclear reaction. The Manhattan Project moved on to other locations, but few people realize that the remains of the first reactor are still buried in Chicagoland.

This first reactor, CP-1, didn't stay in the city long. After two months, Enrico Fermi's experiment moved to a completed research facility at Argonne. The secluded site was built on 1,025 acres of land leased from the Cook County Forest Preserve in Red Gate Woods. The reassembled two-story pile was renamed CP-2. It was joined by CP-3, the world's first water-cooled reactor, in 1944.

After World War II, research continued at Site A by the nation's first nuclear laboratory, Argonne National Laboratory. The reactors were decommissioned in 1954. The land returned to the Forest Preserve, and Argonne moved a few miles away. CP-2 and CP-3 were buried at Site A, and other contaminated materials were buried nearby

---

Why were such dangerous experiments conducted at a university in one of America's largest cities in the first place? Union busting. Argonne's construction was delayed by a strike because non-union labor was being used.

THE WORLD'S FIRST NUCLEAR REACTOR WAS REBUILT AT THIS SITE IN 1943 AFTER INITIAL OPERATION AT THE UNIVERSITY OF CHICAGO THIS REACTOR (CP-2) AND THE FIRST HEAVY WATER MODERATED REACTOR (CP-3) WERE MAJOR FACILITIES AROUND WHICH DEVELOPED THE ARGONNE NATIONAL LABORATORY THIS SITE WAS RELEASED BY THE LABORATORY IN 1956 AND THE U.S. ATOMIC ENERGY COMMISSION THEN BURIED THE REACTORS HERE.

A five-foot-thick concrete radiation shield surrounded the reactor at Site A. The lab was heavily guarded and surrounded by an eight-foot fence topped with barbed wire.

at Plot M. To dispose of the radioactive waste, workers sealed trash like rubber gloves and glass items in containers and buried them in six-foot trenches. No one tracked what was buried.

In the 1970s, low levels of tritium were found in wells at the Red Gate Woods picnic area. Since the levels weren't hazardous to health, it was safer to leave the radioactive remains buried than to risk moving them. In 2002, the Illinois Department of Public Health determined that there was no further public health risk. Both Site A and Plot M are subject to annual monitoring.

The once top-secret area is now accessible to visitors. Start at the Red Gate Woods parking lot and head uphill on a paved trail into the serene woods. Site A lies along the Wolf Road Loop, and Plot M is in a clearing off the Orange Trail. Granite monuments mark these reminders of the sobering power of human ingenuity.

CAIRO CALLING

What message is hidden in these modern hieroglyphics?

King Tut lived more than three thousand years ago, but the discovery of his tomb in 1922 inspired a design craze known as Egyptian Revival. Ancient motifs were found in fashion, artwork, and architecture. Even a warehouse building could be enhanced with a bit of Egyptomania, as evidenced by Reebie Storage and Moving Co.

Styled after ancient Egyptian temples, Reebie's regal building in Lincoln Park looks more like a museum than a warehouse and office. The Clark Street entrance features vibrant terra-cotta sculptures of pharaohs, winged beetles, and lotus leaves. There are even accurate hieroglyphics engraved above the door!

Brothers William and John Reebie founded Reebie Storage and Moving in 1880. They decided to use Egyptian elements in the design of their new warehouse after seeing a storage building in California with a similar style. William and John have left their mark on the building in more ways than one. The two ten-foot-tall Pharaoh Ramses II statues guarding the front door have the Reebie brothers' faces.

The ornate design continues inside. Plaques depict ancient moving scenes, such as Egyptians hauling grain by boat and a Biblical reference to the world's first warehouse. The Egyptian sun god is depicted in the midst of a move. Of course, his servants are doing all the work. The building's

REEBIE STORAGE AND MOVING CO.

WHAT A facade fit for a pharaoh

WHERE 2325 N. Clark St.

COST Free to look, but a move will cost you

PRO TIP Stop by the New Elephant Resale Shop from 12 to 6 p.m. daily to see the building's interior.

Reebie Storage and Moving's seven-story building is one of Chicago's best examples of Egyptian Revival architecture. It's listed on the National Register of Historic Places.

architect worked with Egyptian scholars to make these exact replicas of ancient artwork using plaster casts.

What's the secret to Reebie's longevity? It may have something to do with that hieroglyphic message, which roughly translates to: "I give protection to your furniture" and "Forever I work for all your regions in daylight and darkness." Now that's customer service.

Looking for real ancient artifacts? Visit the Oriental Institute, a free museum and research center located at the University of Chicago. Their collection includes a seventeen-foot-tall statue of King Tutankhamun, a recreation of King Sargon II of Assyria's courtyard, and the largest collection of Mesopotamian materials in the Western Hemisphere.

A HOME RUN LOGO

Did the Chicago Cubs borrow their logo from a Gilded Age gentleman's club?

The Chicago Cubs are one of the most iconic teams in sports, despite their recently broken 108-year streak without a championship. The team conjures up thoughts of ivy and organ music at Wrigley Field, flying the "W" flag after a win, and their distinctive "C" logo. Yet few fans know that the recognizable logo that has adorned the hats of Ernie Banks and Sammy Sosa wasn't quite original.

The Cubs "C" originally stood for the Chicago Athletic Association. The CAA was a private fitness and leisure club for the city's wealthy elite. Founded in 1890, its members included some of Chicago's biggest names, including Marshall Field, A. G. Spalding, and William Wrigley. Wrigley purchased the Cubs, and the organization repurposed the club's crest, a red "C" within a blue circle, for the team logo in 1937.

After sitting vacant for eight years, the Chicago Athletic Association reopened as a 241-room luxury hotel in 2015. These days, you don't have to be among the city's elite to enjoy the property's restaurants and beautifully restored spaces. Visitors to the second-floor Game Room will notice the "C" logo prominently displayed near the indoor bocce

Per *Crain's Chicago Business*, when Cubs owner Tom Ricketts stopped by the hotel in 2015, CAA owner John Pritzker joked, "I assured him he could still use the logo. We wouldn't sue."

CHICAGO ATHLETIC ASSOCIATION

WHAT A design doubleheader

WHERE 12 S. Michigan Ave.

COST Rooms start at $269, but cocktails in the Game Room average around $10.

PRO TIP Stop by the In the Know Desk in the lobby for a free tour of the hotel Monday–Saturday at 2 p.m.

The ranks of CAA's athletes included Olympian and Tarzan actor Johnny Weissmuller, football's first payed player Pudge Heffelfinger, and future corrupt mayor "Big Bill" Thompson. Bottom, CAA's logo was originally black and red. It was changed to red, white, and blue in 1916 as a patriotic response to World War I. Look for the club's old basketball court repurposed as a decorative wall near the bocce ball court. The branded fencing court is now found lining the elevator walls.

court. The club's crest can also be found in original stained glass windows, doorknobs, and flooring throughout the building.

The sports theme is still present in the modern hotel design. Athletic touches include pommel horses used as guest room benches, table legs wrapped in tennis grip, and custom lighting inspired by the lights in the club gym.

Upon its adoption as the symbol of the Cubs, the CAA logo entered a whole new ball game, transforming from representing a privileged few to serving as an emblem for one of the biggest and most devoted fan bases in sports.

21 A ROOM OF ONE'S OWN

Where can I step inside a reclusive artist's bedroom?

Piles of books and paper pour over the tables in this single-room Chicago apartment. Open jars of paint splatter half-finished canvases, while framed religious pictures look down from the walls. You wouldn't imagine this room belonged to a man who was possibly Chicago's most famous artist.

Henry Darger wasn't famous in his lifetime. In fact, few people knew him at all. For most of his life, he was a hospital janitor and dishwasher who lived alone in his Lincoln Park apartment. Shortly before his death in 1973, his landlord cleared out the apartment and discovered a treasure trove of art. Darger's creative output included more than 350 watercolor, pencil, collage, and carbon-traced drawings, seven typewritten hand-bound books, thousands of typewritten sheets, and several journals.

In 2008, Darger's creative work and personal possessions became part of a permanent installation at Intuit: The Center for Intuitive and Outsider Art. The Henry Darger Room Collection is a re-creation of the room he called home for nearly forty years. The space includes his typewriter, tracings, newspaper clippings, cartoons, children's books, coloring books, furniture, and original fixtures.

INTUIT: THE CENTER FOR INTUITIVE AND OUTSIDER ART

WHAT An artist's legacy uncovered

WHERE 756 N. Milwaukee Ave.

COST Voluntary admission is $5; free for members and children under the age of twelve.

NOTEWORTHY Intuit is the only nonprofit organization in the country dedicated solely to presenting self-taught and outsider art.

Henry Darger's living and working space is re-created in this permanent installation. The building he lived in at 851 West Webster Street still stands today, although the neighborhood has been enhanced considerably.

Darger's secret artistic work included a fifteen-thousand-page typewritten fantasy novel called *The Story of the Vivian Girls, in What Is Known as the Realms of the Unreal, of the Glandeco-Angelinian War Storm, Caused by the Child Slave Rebellion*. His painting and collage illustrations depicted the Vivian Girls, child heroines battling evil and oppression. The often-violent depictions of children in his work reflect Darger's own tragic childhood in the foster care system.

After the discovery of his art, Darger's work was celebrated across the world. "I felt really strongly that Darger is arguably Chicago's most famous artist, but many Chicagoans don't know about him," Intuit CEO Debra Kerr told the *Tribune* in 2017. By visiting Darger's re-created personal space, we hope to better understand the secret life of a prolific artist.

According to Intuit, outsider art is produced by self-taught artists from their unique personal visions rather than inspiration from the mainstream art world.

22 SECRET GARDEN

Is Old Town home to a hidden Buddhist garden?

Looking for a little peace in the middle of the city? Old Town has just the place to seek some respite—a serene garden at the Midwest Buddhist Temple.

Everyone is welcome at the Midwest Buddhist Temple, which practices the Jodo Shinshu school of Buddhism. It was founded in 1944 by "resettlers," Japanese Americans who relocated to Chicago after release from World War II internment camps. The present temple was built in 1971.

Located on a quiet street next to a park, the temple is tucked away from the nearby retail and entertainment commotion. "Although we've been part of this community for over seventy years, we're definitely hidden in plain sight," says office manager Jesse Zavala.

In 2014, the temple marked its seventieth anniversary by dedicating a new Legacy Garden. The lush sanctuary is a memorial to the first- and second-generation Japanese Americans (*issei* and *nisei*) who founded the Midwest Buddhist Temple.

Each rock, tree, and shrub in the garden was carefully considered. It took three days to find boulders of the right size and a thirty-ton crane to set them in place. The boulders recall the mountainous setting of sect founder Shinran

MIDWEST BUDDHIST TEMPLE

WHAT An urban oasis

WHERE 435 W. Menomonee St.

COST Free

PRO TIP The Legacy Garden is open to the public the first Sunday of each month, April through November.

Left, *The Legacy Garden was built to honor the founders of the Midwest Buddhist Temple.* Right, *Jodo Shinshu, also known as Shin Buddhism, was founded in Japan. Traditional Buddhism was limited to monastic practice, and Shinran Shonin made Buddhist teachings accessible to ordinary people. More than three hundred million people practice Buddhism worldwide.*

Shonin's walk from Mt. Hiei into the villages as he preached. A trickling stone bowl water feature represents healing. The garden's winding path and the cedar gate's textures and smells are meant to engage all your senses. "The essence is not only a visual effect; it's much more an inner effect," said landscape designer Hoichi Kurisu.

In a city filled with distractions, it's refreshing to savor a space designed for peace and inspiration.

Every August, the temple hosts the Ginza Holiday. The weekend-long cultural festival features Japanese food, music, and artisans.

SUBTERRANEAN CITY

Is Chicago home to an underground labyrinth with a secret symbol?

Chicago's brutally cold winters and scorching summers can make commuting a slog. However, savvy pedestrians escape the extreme weather conditions using a little-known underground network of tunnels called the Pedway.

While tourists and office workers bustle above, a five-mile system of passageways connects forty city blocks just below street level. The Pedway began in 1951 when the city built tunnels connecting the Red and Blue lines at Jackson Boulevard. It has grown over time to include more than fifty public and private buildings connected using tunnels, overhead corridors, and lobbies.

The Pedway is a convenient passageway used by thousands daily, yet most Chicagoans don't know that it exists. Each section of the tunnel is owned and maintained by the building above it, and there's no central department to manage consistency or communications along the system. Pedway maps are outdated and rarely posted. The erratic signage makes this a mysterious maze to the uninitiated.

Some of the Pedway portions allow you to travel both above and below the city streets at once, truly making it a unique Chicago experience. One example of this is the section near the Fairmont Hotel where the Pedway is suspended over an underground portion of East Lake Street but the surface street is above them both.

Left, *One of the Pedway's biggest secrets is how to connect from the warren of tunnels in the Lakeshore East region to the section below Randolph Street's businesses. Enter the South Water Street Metra Station and walk along the train platform to navigate below the Cultural Center.* Right, *This symbol denotes access to the Pedway. Just don't use it as an accurate compass.*

So how do you access the Pedway? Look for its compass symbol posted in buildings and train stations throughout the Loop. Once you see the symbol, you know that underground relief is steps away.

The Pedway is a thriving city under the city. The system connects more than two hundred businesses, including shops and restaurants. Pedestrians can get their nails done, order sushi, and even take a dip in the underground pool at LA Fitness. Cubs announcer Harry Caray went underground for his haircuts at Spa Di La Fronza Salon.

Notice how the Pedway's atmosphere changes as you move between buildings. Some areas are uninspired hallways, while others enjoy bright lighting and public art. Macy's installed a stained glass exhibit in its section, including a piece by Louis Comfort Tiffany!

The tunnels are open when the building above each section is open. The Pedway is not intuitive, but with some patience you'll find a convenient way to bypass traffic downtown and discover a community hidden beneath the streets.

24

ART OF HOUSE

Can I flip through the vinyl collection of the Godfather of House?

In 2004, a portion of Jefferson Street in the West Loop was named the honorary "The Godfather of House Music" Frankie Knuckles Way. The DJ pioneered house music, a form of electronic music with repetitive beats, deep bass, and soul/R&B infusions, at a neighborhood club called the Warehouse in the late 1970s. Knuckles's innovations were the foundation for modern dance and pop music that are thriving today.

Frankie Knuckles passed away in 2014. Fortunately, his musical legacy found a new home at the Stony Island Arts Bank. Chicago artist Theaster Gates purchased the dilapidated former bank from the city for just one dollar to transform it into a gallery, archive, and community center. Frankie Knuckles's collection of five thousand vinyl records is now preserved at the South Shore arts hub and is accessible to the public.

The record collection spans everything from Miles Davis to Mariah Carey. Most records are organized alphabetically, while others are preserved in groupings that Knuckles arranged. Archivists have inventoried the collection, but they haven't cracked the code of the colored dot sticker system Knuckles used to organize it. Even the bags he used to carry his vinyl tell a story through their stamps from countries around the world.

The Stony Island Trust & Savings Bank was built in 1923. It was added to the National Register of Historic Places in 2013.

Make a reservation to flip through Frankie Knuckles's collection of five thousand records. The music that belonged to the Godfather of House Music is one of several cultural collections at the Stony Island Arts Bank.

STONY ISLAND ARTS BANK

WHAT An artful investment

WHERE 6760 S. Stony Island Ave.

COST Free

PRO TIP Access to the collections requires a free thirty-minute library orientation, hosted daily at 2:00 p.m. Reservations are required to view the Frankie Knuckles vinyl collection.

In addition to the Knuckles collection, the Arts Bank features galleries of curated art. Other collections include the library and archives of Johnson Publishing, publisher of iconic African American magazines like *Ebony* and *Jet*. The Edward J. Williams Collection has assembled four thousand objects of "negrobilia," objects depicting stereotypical images of people of color, to remove them from circulation. The bank is also home to the University of Chicago's sixty-thousand-slide collection of art and architectural history.

Around the world, this beloved artist's music keeps spinning. It's fitting that Frankie Knuckles's tools reside in a bank where the currency is community.

25

NO BONES ABOUT IT

Where can I shop for taxidermy and tintypes?

Chicago's most distinctive antique store got its start far away in the hills of Transylvania. Inspired by a trip tracing the footsteps of Vlad the Impaler, Adam and Skye Rust decided to bring their love of travel home to Chicago. They opened Woolly Mammoth Chicago Antiques & Oddities in 2010, stocking it with the weirdest finds from the Midwest and around the world.

Are you in the market for Ecuadorian shrunken heads? How about Victorian mourning jewelry made from human hair? Is your living room calling out for a display of bat skeletons or snakes in a jar? Woolly Mammoth specializes in bizarre animal and medical ephemera, among other peculiar treasures. The owners scour flea markets, estate sales, and auctions across the globe to procure the items that line their walls.

The Rusts don't simply display found objects— they give them new life by combining them to create art. A stuffed alligator has become a lamp with a bulb in its mouth. An oversized wiener dog wears a red velvet tuxedo and cummerbund and plays the violin, becoming "Fiddler on the Woof."

So many taxidermy enthusiasts have found a home in Woolly Mammoth that the Andersonville shop began

WOOLLY MAMMOTH CHICAGO ANTIQUES & ODDITIES

WHAT Chicago's curiosity cabinet

WHERE 1513 W. Foster Ave.

COST Dental slides will run you $3 and a camel skull is $545.

PRO TIP Items change daily, so stop by often to get your oddity fix.

Woolly Mammoth is home to a collection of two-headed taxidermy animals. It's the only place in Chicago where you can see a two-headed turtle or a cat with two bodies but one head.

offering periodic taxidermy classes. Beginners can learn how to bring animals like pheasants back to life with the art of taxidermy.

It's easy to see death among the store's mounted animals and stockpiles of teeth, but Woolly Mammoth lives in the present. "This is all still a celebration of life," Skye Rust told *Time Out Chicago*. "We're giving [dead animals] an afterlife of a sort."

Whether or not your home needs a conversation piece like a two-headed cow or a wooden peg leg from the 1850s, you'll enjoy sifting through Woolly Mammoth's collection— we're dead certain.

The creepiest item in Woolly Mammoth's collection? A caricature of Adolf Hitler believed to be drawn and signed by serial killer John Wayne Gacy.

26

EXCREMENT AS ART

Why is there a poop-shaped sculpture in Ukrainian Village?

Art can convey a powerful message, and one artist in Ukrainian Village has raised awareness for his cause by putting poo on a pedestal. Since 2005, a residence at the corner of Augusta Boulevard and Wolcott Avenue has featured a giant bronze coil of crap in its yard.

This metallic mound sits proudly on a three-foot sandstone column bearing the name *Shit Fountain* on all four sides. The bronze bowel movement gently trickles water into a basin.

Chicago artist Jerzy S. Kenar created and installed the fountain on his property with a specific message in mind. It's a playful reminder to dog owners in the community to pick up after their pooches.

After one too many instances of doggie defecation in his garden, Kenar went a step beyond posting the typical handwritten notice in his yard. As he told *Time Out Chicago*, "I have flowers in front of the gallery, and someone [will be] walking their dog and the dog is jumping there . . . and shitting there and someone is not picking [it] up."

While it may not be everybody's idea of neighborhood beautification, the sculpture is meant to be a lighthearted, humorous reminder. A dog owner himself, Kenar erected the artwork as a tribute to all Chicago canines.

SHIT FOUNTAIN

WHAT A powerful reminder to pick up after your pets

WHERE 1001 N. Wolcott Ave.

COST Free

PRO TIP BYO doggie waste bag.

Left, *This sculpture is more than neighborhood art—it's a public service announcement.* Right, *Kenar Studio, located on the same property, is a neighborhood treasure brimming with whimsical artwork. Kenar is best known for his religious and political artworks, which include those displayed at Loyola University's Madonna della Strada Chapel and the Holy Trinity Polish Mission in Chicago.*

In the years since its installation, the fountain has become an unlikely local favorite. It's not uncommon to see visitors posing for pictures with the fountain or confusing it with an oversized poo emoji. In a city brimming with art, Kenar and his feces fountain have made quite a mark.

The internationally renowned artist's work also includes pieces at O'Hare Airport, the Harold Washington Library, and the Black History Fountain at Renaissance Park.

27 CIRCUS CATASTROPHE

How did Forest Park become the final resting place for a doomed circus caravan?

Chicagoland is home to many unusual graveyards, but none so distinctive as the Showmen's Rest plot at Woodlawn Cemetery in Forest Park, Illinois. It is the burial place for circus performers and other outdoor amusement veterans who have seen their last curtain call.

The Showmen's League purchased the plot as a resting place for their members in 1917. They couldn't have known that the plot would be used the following year to bury victims of one of circus history's greatest tragedies.

On July 21, 1918, the Hagenbeck-Wallace Circus wrapped up a show in Michigan City, Indiana, as part of their Midwest tour. Three trains carried twenty-two tents, four hundred animals, one thousand employees, and equipment overnight to their next show in Hammond, Indiana. The company was scheduled to parade through town the following day, promoting the feats and fancies of the big top. But no one would be celebrating.

Mechanical trouble stopped the train in its tracks with performers, families, and roustabouts onboard. In the dead of night, another train slammed into the circus train from behind at full speed. The train burst into flames, crushing or

Founded in 1913 in Chicago, the Showmen's League counted Buffalo Bill Cody as its first president. The organization is still headquartered in Chicago today.

Reports of phantom animal noises on the property led to legends of ghostly circus animals haunting the cemetery. The rumors were put to rest when the sounds were traced back to nearby Brookfield Zoo. No elephants were killed in the crash or buried in the cemetery.

trapping many of the sleeping passengers under mangled steel and wood.

Days after the accident, fifty-six of the victims were buried at Woodlawn Cemetery. Many of these employees were temporary workers and their legal names were unknown. Headstones were marked with nicknames like "Baldy" or simply "Unknown Male."

Five elephant sculptures watch over the fallen performers and the hundreds of others who have joined them. The elephants' trunks are lowered in a traditional sign of mourning. Consummate showmen to the last, the Hagenbeck-Wallace Circus resumed performances days after the memorial service. As they say, the show must go on.

28

HOLLYWOOD MOMENT

Was Chicago the first Hollywood?

Lights, camera . . . Uptown? When Los Angeles was a distant backwater, Chicago spent a decade as the center of the world's film industry. You can still find remnants of the city's historic movie magic if you know where to look.

Essanay Studios was the Warner Brothers of the early twentieth century. Its name comes from the combined surname initials of George Spoor and Gilbert "Bronco Billy" Anderson, who formed the studio in 1907. Essanay's silent film stars included screen queen Gloria Swanson, cross-eyed comic Ben Turpin, and heartthrob Francis X. Bushman.

The studio's biggest luminary was Charlie Chaplin. The world's top box-office star worked at Essanay from 1915 to 1916. The Little Tramp produced fourteen films for Essanay, although only *His New Job* was shot in Chicago. Gloria Swanson was an uncredited extra on the film, appearing as a stenographer.

Nearby, in present-day North Center, William Selig founded the largest film studio ever built at the time. Constructed in 1896, the Selig Polyscope complex took up a

---

Selig Polyscope's main building at 3900 North Claremont Avenue still stands. Look for the studio's logo, an "S" inside a diamond, above the main entrance. They shot outdoor films in the middle of the block, so it wasn't unusual for neighbors to spot actors in Civil War or Wild West dress.

The building to the east contains the Charlie Chaplin Auditorium, a former sound stage dedicated by the university and now used for events. Occasionally visitors have the opportunity to see a film shot by Essanay in this very room!

city block. Selig created some of the first full-length feature films and made the first *Wizard of Oz* films in 1907.

Chicago's cinematic golden age was unceremoniously ended by patent litigation and . . . the weather. Selig Polyscope established Southern California's first permanent movie studio, and much of the industry headed west. Chicago just couldn't compete with California's mild, year-round shooting weather. As the *Los Angeles Times* reported in 1916, Charlie Chaplin returned to California because Chicago was "too damn cold."

Today, one of the Selig Polyscope structures survives as a condo building. Two of Essanay's red brick buildings, now home to St. Augustine College, commemorate Chicago's film heyday. The studio's name appears in terra-cotta above the western building's entrance and is guarded by Essanay's trademark Native Americans. It may be two thousand miles from the Walk of Fame, but you can still trace the footsteps of movie stars in Chicago!

29

BUZZING ALONG

Why does a hive of bees live in a Michigan Avenue hotel?

The beverage world is buzzing, and the reason is on the rooftop of a downtown Chicago hotel. Given the prices of Streeterville real estate, it's surprising to find that the Marriott's top spot is inhabited by . . . swarms of bees?

These are just a few of the hives owned by Wild Blossom Meadery & Winery founder, Greg Fischer. You might remember mead as the drink of choice for mythic warrior types like Beowulf and Thor, but the ancient honey wine is regaining popularity today.

When Fischer founded Wild Blossom in 2001, it was the first meadery in Illinois and the first winery in Chicago. In 2016, it was one of three hundred meaderies nationwide, according to the American Mead Makers Association.

Part of mead's appeal is its local origin. As Fischer says, "Mead is like nature in a glass." Wild Blossom makes all its mead with honey produced in the Chicago area and Lake Michigan water. Fischer and his employees tend 125 bee colonies everywhere from the Morton Arboretum to the former US Steel mills site at 87th Street. After the honey is collected, it's extracted from the comb by spinning in a centrifuge, thinned with water,

---

WILD BLOSSOM MEADERY & WINERY

WHAT Nature in a glass

WHERE 9030 S. Hermitage Ave.

COST Tastings start at $2; a flight of six meads is $10.

PRO TIP Don't miss the wine selection, including bottles like Chicago South Side shiraz and Chicago Bull's Blood blend.

Left, *Wild Blossom's facility includes a tasting room, an educational area for brewing and winemaking classes, and an outdoor patio along the Dan Ryan Woods.* Right, *According to Fischer, Wild Blossom's bees pollinate around two million flowers, producing twenty to forty million seeds for new flowers.*

and fermented at Wild Blossom's nine-thousand-square-foot facility in Beverly.

Meads range from sweet to dry, and Wild Blossom makes about two dozen types of mead. In addition to meads infused with local fruits, they serve twists like Sweet Desire, a bourbon-barrel-aged mead, and Pirate's Blood, infused with chili peppers.

Chicagoans like to eat and drink local, but few realize that one of the region's most distinct local beverages is tucked away in the city's southwest corner. Every kind of flower produces different flavored honey, and each honey produces a different mead, so you can say cheers to Chicago's worker bees with a new flavor on each visit.

Mead is believed to be the oldest alcoholic beverage, predating beer and grape wine by thousands of years. Pottery vessels found in northern China contain remnants of fermented honey and rice dating from 6500–7000 BC.

30

AN EXPLOSIVE LAWN ORNAMENT

Why is a World War I cannon on display in a Wicker Park yard?

A stroll through Wicker Park's leafy historic district offers views of Victorian-era homes just steps from the vibrant "six corners" intersection. One yellow Queen Anne mansion in particular turns heads, but people may be reacting to the 2,600-pound cannon displayed in its front yard.

Built in 1912, the 4.7-inch howitzer was used for training during World War I. The cannon never served overseas, but it's rumored to have guarded Navy Pier during the war. Today it rests quietly on a 1918 Studebaker caisson.

So how did a weapon of war end up on this quiet street? The cannon officially belongs to the Naval Station Great Lakes, located thirty miles north of the home. The house became an American Legion Hall in the 1920s, and the cannon was added to mark the charter of American Legion Pulaski Post 86 in 1934. It even witnessed President Truman's visit to the hall in 1951.

The American Legion closed in 1972, and the Sommers family has called the building and its historic cannon home since 1977. "We have seen cars almost rear-ended when one would slam on the brakes as they took a double-take,"

The last Chicago home of celebrated writer Nelson Algren is also in the neighborhood. The author of *The Man with the Golden Arm* lived at 1958 West Evergreen Avenue from 1959 to 1975.

This historic part of Wicker Park was referred to as "Beer Baron's Row" in the nineteenth century. You can still admire the mansions of wealthy German and Scandinavian brewers on Hoyne Avenue and Pierce Street.

WICKER PARK CANNON

WHAT A piece of World War I history in plain sight

WHERE 1558 N. Hoyne Ave.

COST Free

PRO TIP Visitors are welcome to admire the cannon and plaque from the sidewalk, but this is a private residence.

owner Carol Summers said. "The main response from onlookers is, 'Why it is there?'"

But the cannon hadn't seen its last battle. A legionnaire asked to add the cannon to his post in DeKalb, Illinois. The Sommers family and the Old Wicker Park Committee resisted, and Great Lakes agreed it should remain where it had stood watch for decades. The family even received a letter from former US representative Dan Rostenkowski stating that the cannon belongs in front of the home. It turns out that Rostenkowski's father was a leader at Pulaski Post 86!

When the legionnaire came to take the cannon away, Carol Sommers defended her post with the letter. It was never a hero abroad, but the Wicker Park cannon earned high honors in neighborhood lore.

31 SAVED FROM THE WRECKING BALL

Does a demolished architectural treasure live inside the Art Institute?

With 1.5 million annual visitors, the Art Institute of Chicago is hardly a secret. Yet many who stumble on an elegant, empty room tucked on the museum's east side have no idea they've entered an icon.

This room was originally built in 1894 as part of the Chicago Stock Exchange by the famed team of Louis Sullivan and Dankmar Adler. The frenzied forces in this room controlled national meat and vegetable commodities as the shouts of "Buy!" and "Sell!" rang throughout. A 1960 *Chicago Tribune* report described how "the shouts of the white coated, gray coated, and tan coated men clustered about the big, horseshoe shaped desks below" conveyed a sense of "excitement and tension."

The building was slated for demolition in 1972, and preservationists took action. The Art Institute agreed to reconstruct the Trading Room in a new wing. Photographer Richard Nickel, architect John Vinci, and others spent months documenting the room and salvaging what remained of its decorative fragments. Tragically, Nickel died in an accident at the Stock Exchange demolition site, and he never saw the completed reconstruction of the room he fought to save.

The room contains fifteen distinct stenciled patterns. The most complex pattern contains fifty-two different colors.

Although Chicago lost the Stock Exchange Building to demolition, its magnificent Trading Room is preserved in a quiet corner of the Art Institute.

Today, the Trading Room is reflective space to admire the sublime details that were almost lost. The colorful stenciling was restored one square inch at a time to reveal intricate, organic patterns that set the room in motion. Ornate stained glass skylights glow around the perimeter of the two-story coffered ceiling. Looking at the massive chalkboard, you can imagine traders shouting prices across the room.

The Chicago Stock Exchange Trading Room is a grand example of Chicago's pioneering modern design legacy. Thanks to Chicago's preservationists, this craftsmanship has a home among the rest of the Art Institute's world-renowned collection.

CHICAGO STOCK EXCHANGE TRADING ROOM

WHAT A historic room reconstructed

WHERE 111 S. Michigan Ave.

COST Admission is $25 for adults, $19 for students and seniors, and free for children under fourteen.

PRO TIP The Chicago Stock Exchange's terra-cotta entrance arch is also preserved at the Art Institute. Look for it along the east side of the museum near Monroe Street.

AS SEEN ON TV

Where does Chicago's movie magic come from?

Chances are, when you're watching a film set in the past, you don't think twice about where all that old stuff on the set comes from. Yet once you've visited Zap Props's 36,000-square-foot warehouse, you won't be able to stop looking for their artifacts on the big screen.

Zap Props collects thousands of items, from the remarkable to the mundane, and rents them as props for movies, TV, theater, and more. You may have seen some of Zap's collection featured in *Transformers*, *Home Alone*, *Batman: The Dark Knight*, and *Chicago Fire*. They also fabricate props for others from their workshop and provide the decorations for restaurants like Tilted Kilt and Giordano's.

A commonplace Bridgeport industrial corridor seems an unlikely location for the treasure trove inside Chicago's largest prop house. From the outside, you'd never know that Zap's three-story warehouse contains vintage gas pumps and walls covered in sharks. Owner Bill Rawski estimates that there are about a million items in Zap's collection.

Zap Props specializes in items from the 1920s through the 1970s. So, if you need a 1940s kitchen set complete

---

It pays to collect in big quantities. One scene in the film *The Road to Perdition* required different kinds of whiskey barrels. Zap Props rented the film eighty to one hundred barrels for the production.

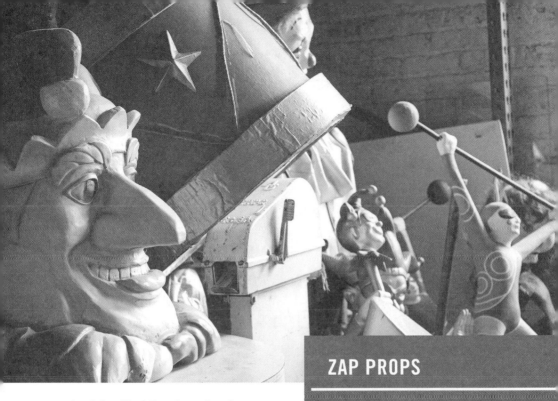

Look familiar? Zap Props has been featured in an episode of American Pickers.

ZAP PROPS

WHAT Hollywood's garage

WHERE 3611 S. Loomis Pl.

COST Available upon request

PRO TIP Visits are by appointment only.

with canned goods or a vintage Art Deco barber shop, you're in luck. The inventory is organized by type and age. Items cover the space, from aisles crammed with carousel horses to an astronaut suit hanging from the ceiling.

Bringing history to life is a family business. Rawski's son and daughter also work at Zap Props. They source most of their items from Chicagoland's auctions and flea markets. Chicago's legacy as a manufacturing hotspot makes it a great place to unearth items made here, like vintage Zenith radios.

If your next event could use an eye-catching centerpiece, a gold throne, or a 1957 Chevy convertible, it may be waiting for you in Bridgeport.

33 THE LEANING TOWER OF NILES

How did an iconic Italian replica end up in Illinois?

Can't make it to Italy anytime soon? Not to worry, there's a piece of Pisa just outside Chicago. The village of Niles, Illinois, is the unlikely home of a half-size reproduction of the famous leaning tower.

In the 1930s, local businessman Robert Ilg decided that the best way to camouflage the building of a dull water tower was to wrap it in a landmark look-alike. Ilg needed a water filtration tank to supply outdoor swimming pools in a private park he was building. He disguised it as the Leaning Tower of Pisa to maintain the area's natural beauty. He also wanted to pay tribute to Galileo, the esteemed astronomer and Pisa native who performed physics experiments at the Tower of Pisa.

Completed in 1934, the tower is half the size of its Pisa predecessor. The structure is 94 feet tall and it leans 7.4 feet, compared to the 177-foot height and 13-foot lean of the original. Where Pisa has unstable sand and clay, Niles has reinforced concrete and a San Francisco engineering team to keep its lean consistent.

The tower was later donated to the Niles YMCA and leased to the village. Although it's six hundred years younger than the original tower, its age began to show. The tower experienced a $1.2 million renovation in the 1990s,

---

The village of Niles and Pisa, Italy,
became sister cities in 1991.

A plaque at Leaning Tower Plaza dedicates the structure to "all who contribute and strive to make this Earth and its unlimited resources, materially and scientifically a better place for mankind."

THE LEANING TOWER OF NILES

WHAT A replica of Pisa's tipsy tower

WHERE 6300 Touhy Ave., Niles, IL

COST Free

NOTEWORTHY The tower's top floor contains bells imported from Italy.

which included the addition of a plaza with fountains, a reflecting pool, and a "telefono" booth. Recent proposals have suggested turning the area around the tower into a cultural destination and hosting live music events in the plaza.

The tower has become a local landmark and a roadside attraction for curious drivers on Touhy Avenue. There's no consensus yet on whether Niles is indeed the Italy of the Midwest.

34 THE CURIOUS COUCH TOMB

Why is there a mausoleum in Lincoln Park and who is buried there?

Before Lincoln Park became grounds for leisure, it was a burial ground for Chicago's dead. The area served as Chicago City Cemetery until the city decided to convert it in 1866. The bodies were relocated to newer facilities like Graceland and Rosehill Cemeteries. Yet one tomb is still visible in the park, and its inhabitants carried their identity to the grave.

Chicago hotelier Ira Couch was interred at the south end of Lincoln Park in 1858. The tomb, built by his brother James, cost seven thousand dollars, which was a small fortune at the time. The stately vault contained space for eleven bodies.

So why did Ira's remains remain in the park when other bodies were moved? Some accounts suggest that the Couch family threatened to sue the city or that the cost of moving the tomb was too steep.

The mystery of the vault's contents was first raised when James Couch died in 1892. Supposedly, he could not join his brother to rest in the tomb because the door rusted shut. Cemetery records were lost by this time, and firsthand accounts of who was actually inside the tomb varied. Some friends and relatives claimed Ira alone rested in the vault. Conflicting accounts believe that up to seven Couch

Victims of the Great Chicago Fire took refuge in City Cemetery's open graves, which were dug up to relocate the occupants.

68

Although Couch's tomb is the only grave marker left in Lincoln Park, not all the remains were moved. It's estimated that up to twelve thousand bodies are still buried under the park grounds. Dozens of skeletons were discovered as recently as 1998.

relatives are buried there, including Ira's parents, children, or grandchildren.

Adding to the confusion, the Couch monument at the family's subsequent Rosehill Cemetery plot lists Ira and his parents. However, they are not mentioned in the Rosehill lot card. There is no record of if and when the inhabitants of the Couch tomb were ever moved there.

The Couch family built a tomb to stand the test of time, and a mystery to go along with it. While we may never know who rests inside, the mausoleum is a reminder of Lincoln Park's history as a resting place for Chicagoans.

35 SWEET TOOTH

Why does downtown Chicago smell like chocolate?

Many Chicagoans know that the city is named after a smell. *Chicagoua* is the Miami and Illinois peoples' word for the "wild leek" that grew abundantly on the banks of the Chicago River. For years, the city's smells came from manufacturing grit or the ripe scent of the Union Stockyards. But if you're anywhere near the West Loop, chances are the sweet smell of chocolate fills the air.

Visitors passing under the Kinzie Street Bridge on boat tours often think the tantalizing smell must be in their heads, and even longtime residents can't locate the source of the brownie-like aroma. Chicago's sweet secret floats out of a brick building on West Kinzie Street that houses the Blommer Chocolate factory.

Blommer Chocolate was founded in 1939 by three brothers. The business was run by four generations of chocolate makers until it was sold in 2018. Blommer is the largest cocoa processor and ingredient chocolate supplier in North America. It produces cocoa powder and butter, coatings, and other products for candy manufacturers.

The chocolate aroma even inspired its own tracker. In 2014, a technologist created a map to report the smell's daily reach using the National Weather Service's wind report, historical reports, and crowdsourcing. Although the site is now defunct, here's hoping someone will revive it.

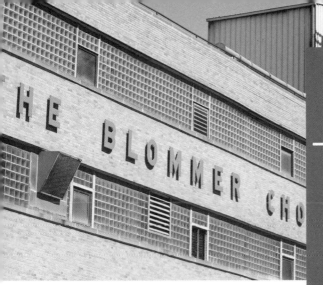

BLOMMER CHOCOLATE COMPANY

WHAT Chicago's sweetest smell

WHERE 600 W. Kinzie St.

COST Free brownie smells courtesy of your friendly neighborhood candy maker

PRO TIP Enjoy a picnic with a side of sweet scent across the street in Fulton River Park.

A fire that broke out in the factory on New Year's Day in 1980 literally turned the place to hot chocolate. Per the Chicago Tribune, *"Chocolate melted and formed puddles big enough to wade in, three feet deep and 30 feet wide.*

The source of Chicago's chocolate scent? Blommer's roasting cocoa beans. The epicenter of the confectionary fragrance is the factory's location between Halsted Street and the Chicago River. However, it has been sniffed all the way east to Michigan Avenue, as far north as Oak Street, and south to the Loop.

There is at least one person in the city who isn't enticed by cocoa in the air. In 2005, a citizen complaint led to a citation by the Environmental Protection Agency for excessive emissions of cocoa dust from Blommer's cocoa bean grinders. Blommer responded by installing equipment to reduce emissions. Fortunately, the chocolate smell was reduced but not removed from the city's smellscape. So the next time you're scurrying to the train or office, don't forget to stop and smell the chocolate.

36

THE HIDDEN GALLERY

Are priceless works of art displayed in a Chicago Park District fieldhouse?

One of the best collections of fine arts by Chicago-area artists is in an unlikely location. To view the Vanderpoel Art Collection, you'll have to head to a Chicago Park District fieldhouse.

John Vanderpoel's name is familiar on the Southwest Side. Beverly is home to a street and an elementary school named in his honor. Born Johannes van der Poel, the artist emigrated to the United States from the Netherlands in 1869. When the art world came to Chicago during the 1893 World's Columbian Exposition, Vanderpoel exhibited five paintings at the fair and helped jury fine arts.

Vanderpoel was best known as an educator, and he taught at the Art Institute for thirty years. His 1907 book on figure drawing, *The Human Figure*, was a standard textbook for art schools, and it remains in print today. One of his many students was Georgia O'Keeffe, who referred to Vanderpoel in her autobiography as "one of the few real teachers I have known."

VANDERPOEL ART MUSEUM

WHAT A priceless art collection

WHERE 9625 S. Longwood Dr.

COST Free

NOTEWORTHY Vanderpoel's Beverly home at 9319 S. Pleasant Ave. is still standing.

The collection of about 660 paintings, drawings, and sculptures is considered one of the largest holdings of American impressionism in the Midwest. Amazingly, the impressive collection was all donated! After Vanderpoel's death, former students and other artists who admired him contributed pieces to a memorial collection. Works by Grant Wood, Maxfield Parrish, Mary Cassatt, James McNeill Whistler, and Frank W. Benson hang next to Vanderpoels.

About 186 of the Vanderpoel Art Collection's most notable pieces are on display in the Ridge Park Fieldhouse.

The John H. Vanderpoel Art Association is in residency at Ridge Park through the Chicago Park District's Arts Partners in Residence Program, which unites artists and communities in Chicago's parks.

"Even longtime neighbors are stunned when they look at the room. They didn't know it was here," says collection historian Sidney Hamper. Today, the association seeks to maintain the collection, restoring about seven pictures each year. Unbeknownst to most Chicagoans, the modest second-floor room of the Ridge Park fieldhouse hides a priceless collection.

No one is sure whether the area was named after Beverly, Massachusetts, or Beverly Hills, California, but many residents call the neighborhood "Beverly Hills." It's one of Chicago's only hilly areas. In fact, a glacial ridge just west of Longwood Drive is the highest point in Chicago.

37

NO-FLY ZONE

Was the dome on top of the InterContinental Hotel built for blimps?

In a sea of Chicago skyscrapers, you're sure to recognize the InterContinental Chicago. It's the one crowned with a gold onion-shaped dome just north of the Chicago River. Legend has it that this dome was built to dock airships in the dirigible age, but did they ever land?

The Shriners built the forty-two-story tower in 1929 as the Medinah Athletic Club. The extravagant design included elements from far-flung cultures including Assyrian, Greek, medieval English, Egyptian, and Mesopotamian. Amenities included a shooting range, bowling alley, boxing arena, and a twenty-third-floor miniature golf course complete with water hazards and a wandering brook.

The building's golden cupola was designed with a chimney and extension pole to moor airships. A 1929 photo in the Art Institute's collection even shows a zeppelin flying near the dome with this caption: "Count Dr. Eckener and his Zeppelin visits our club by air." However, no airship ever moored to the roof of any building in the country. Although zeppelin masts provided great publicity for tall buildings, they were never practical or safe in practice.

The dome does conceal a secret. Beneath it on the forty-second-floor rooftop, a small lounge and outdoor terrace provide dizzying views of downtown. The rooftop isn't

INTERCONTINENTAL CHICAGO

WHAT A secret in the sky

WHERE 505 N. Michigan Ave.

COST Rooms start at $199.

PRO TIP A secret tour allows you to explore the hotel's grand design for free. Ask for the iPod tour at the concierge desk.

Left, *The Medinah Athletic Club's design referenced styles from all over the world in rooms such as King Arthur's Court, the Renaissance Ballroom, and the Spanish Court. The Grand Ballroom's twelve-thousand-pound Baccarat crystal chandelier was once the largest in North America.* Right, *While the rest of the hotel underwent a painstaking restoration in the 1980s, the fourteenth-floor pool remained pristine. Soak in the pool's Spanish tiles, marble pillars, stained glass windows, and fountain of Neptune.*

open to the public, but you can rent the thirty-second-floor Tower Lounge and guest rooms to get to new heights.

While most visitors won't be accessing the InterContinental observatory, there's another way to dive into history at the hotel. The opulent pool on the fourteenth floor was the first built at such a height. Rows of seats hearken to when swimming was a spectator sport. If the likes of Esther Williams and *Tarzan* actor Johnny Weissmuller swam in your pool, who wouldn't watch?

The athletic club's 1930 yearbook, the *Scimitar,* guided the $30 million restoration work. Its black-and-white photographs were used to duplicate and restore entire rooms. The yearbook and other club memorabilia are on display in a small hotel museum called the Cornerstone.

38

GROUND CONTROL

Is there such a thing as a pretty pothole?

Imagine navigating your car or bike down one of Chicago's pothole-ridden streets—swerving here, jostling there. Then something catches your eye. Instead of your tire hitting another hole, it glides by a mosaic of the Chicago flag. Where did *that* come from?

You can thank local artist Jim Bachor for transforming dozens of Chicago's infrastructure craters into public art. Since 2013, he's taken his skills as a mosaic artist to the streets to fill potholes with art instead of asphalt. His concrete crusade began after a pothole in front of his North Side home just never got repaired. Bachor explains, "I merged my passion for an artform that's so durable with a problem that can never be fixed long term."

Where most people see reminders of a long winter gouged into the pavement, Jim sees a canvas. Bachor's playful depictions include the Chicago flag, ice cream treats, and floral bouquets. One tile mosaic simply spells "pothole."

Bachor's methods aren't so different from ancient mosaic artists. He finds a pothole near the edge of the street that isn't too big or shallow. He creates the marble and art glass mosaic in his studio over about eight hours. When the weather is right, Bachor sports a safety vest and sets up orange traffic cones at the site. The process of mixing the

---

City crews filled 40,262 potholes in January 2016, according to the Tribune. That's down from 94,307 in January 2014.

Jim Bachor finds beauty in the everyday, like a bag of Cheetos. His Chicago work includes the Thrive *mosaic at the CTA Thorndale Red Line station and works at the Nike store on Michigan Avenue and Pork and Mindy's restaurant in Wicker Park. He has installed pothole mosaics as far away as Finland.*

POTHOLE ART

WHAT Picturesque pavement

WHERE Various

COST A harsh winter

PRO TIP Hunt for pothole art with Bachor's map of installations at bachor.com. Note that potholes may be covered or destroyed.

concrete, filling the pothole, and installing the mosaic takes a few hours. The next day, he scrubs the mosaic clean. Bachor uses social media to leave a photo clue to the location of each new installation along with a goody bag.

While the Department of Transportation doesn't condone guerilla pothole repair, they can't deny the delight of Bachor's work. As a representative told the *Tribune* in 2014, "Mr. Bachor and his art are proof that even the coldest, harshest winter cannot darken the spirits of Chicagoans."

39

A CUT ABOVE

Where can I see a collection of ancient trephined skulls?

The idea of a mad scientist conjures up images of tools, potions, and experiments that are better left in fiction than on the modern operating table. However, these grisly depictions have a basis in centuries of medical history. You can explore the intersection of medical science, art, and history at the International Museum of Surgical Science.

You don't need a medical background to appreciate the delightfully creepy collection. The museum's permanent holdings include medical artifacts, fine art, a library, and a manuscript collection. Rotating exhibits cover everything from synesthesia to gender transition. Where else can you see an iron lung, letters by Florence Nightingale, and replicas of surgical instruments salvaged from Pompeii?

Throughout the museum, more than six hundred paintings and sculptures depict notable medical figures or harrowing surgical scenes in history. Stop by the contemporary art galleries for a modern interpretation. The fine art collection includes a plaster cast made in 1821 from Napoleon's death mask.

The museum's location in a four-story lakeshore mansion is a Chicago secret in its own right. It was built in 1917 for socialite Eleanor Robinson Countiss, and it is the only Gold

---

Chicago-born Dr. Max Thorek founded the International College of Surgeons in 1935 in Geneva. His goal was to promote exchange between surgeons. It's still located next door to the museum.

The only museum dedicated to medical surgery in North America was founded in 1954 by Dr. Max Thorek. The collection of more than seven thousand artifacts from cultures across the world shows the evolution of surgery through centuries, from bloodletting to modern germ theory.

INTERNATIONAL MUSEUM OF SURGICAL SCIENCE

WHAT A macabre collection of medical history

WHERE 1524 N. Lake Shore Dr.

COST Adults $15, students and seniors $12, children $8, under three free

PRO TIP Don't miss the gift shop if you're in the market for a spine pen or stuffed microbe.

Coast mansion open to the public. The impressive abode was designed to resemble Le Petit Trianon, Marie Antoinette's playhouse at Versailles. Today, five thousand rare medical books line the walls of the former billiard room. The gilded staircase and marble floors are quite a contrast to the more morbid pieces on exhibit.

It's fascinating to walk through the unfolding story of medicine and innovation. While we all have a bone to pick with modern healthcare, there's no doubt we're better off today. Here's wondering what contemporary surgical practices will find a home in the museum for future generations!

40 ALL DOLLED UP

What can you find in Jojo's Closet?

This nondescript brick building conceals a fantasyland turned to life. Here, dolls have a heart, there's a different face for every evening, and club kids remain kids at heart. Welcome to Jojo's Closet.

Jojo Baby is a Chicago artist, drag performer, and legendary nightlife personality. Entering his studio, crammed with handmade dolls, cast phallus artwork, a Raggedy Ann collection, and pairs of sparkly red shoes, is like stepping into a world of pure imagination.

This studio is where Jojo Baby creates dolls, puppets, jewelry, costumes, and paintings. Jojo's craftsmanship was inspired by his late friend and mentor, transgender artist Greer Lankton, who worked in Andy Warhol's Factory and for Jim Henson.

Jojo's bendable dolls resemble friends or icons like Divine and Marilyn Monroe. They're sculpted with a full skeleton from wood, wire, and plastic. They often include real human teeth and hair. Each doll is crafted with a full chakra system and a crystal heart christened with voodoo love oil so that "if they ever leave me someone will love them as much as I do."

Jojo Baby doesn't just make art, he *lives* it. He started as a beautician and was one of Chicago's original club kids. He

---

Jojo Baby's first studio was in an actual broom closet in Wicker Park's Flat Iron Building. His current studio is at the Rot Shop, an effects, scenic, and prop shop.

Jojo Baby hopes to someday create a doll museum from his extensive collection, which includes pre-Columbian, cornhusk, resin, and voodoo dolls. He's drawn to dolls because "they're always there and they never lie."

JOJO'S CLOSET

WHAT Valley of the dolls

WHERE 2546 W. Chicago Ave.

COST Free

PRO TIP Check the Rot Shop's Facebook page for upcoming events or to contact Jojo Baby to visit his studio by appointment.

became known for an ability to transform week to week in showstopping visual personas. "When I dress up, I call it putting on the goddess," Jojo says.

In addition to transforming himself for each event, Jojo Baby works as a stylist for celebrities. Do you remember Dennis Rodman's wild hairstyles in the late 1990s? Jojo Baby was responsible for the Chicago Bull's distinctive leopard and camouflage hair.

With so many personas to share, it's no surprise that Jojo Baby has been the subject of two documentaries, including one by his idol, *Hellraiser* director Clive Barker. As Jojo says, "I'm like a ball of clay, I can change."

41 'TIL DEATH DO US PART

Did a young bride send messages from beyond the grave?

Mount Carmel Cemetery is the final resting place for many powerful Chicagoans, from archbishops to the more notorious Dean O'Banion and Al Capone. Yet only one resident has the power to communicate with the living after death.

The life-sized marble statue at Julia Buccola's grave was not the site's original marker. Her family erected the likeness of a bride holding a bouquet only after Julia asked to be exhumed.

Julia's family immigrated to the West Side of Chicago from Sicily after their father's death. In 1920, she married Matthew Petta at Holy Rosary Parish. She died in childbirth about nine months later and was buried in her wedding gown holding her stillborn child.

Julia's mother, Filomena, began having recurring nightmares after her daughter's death. She claimed that Julia told her she was buried alive and wanted to be free. Filomena attempted to have her body exhumed for six years, and finally prevailed. In 1927, the casket was unearthed and opened.

The contents shocked everyone. Julia's body had not decomposed, although the body of her infant son had. A photograph taken at the time shows Julia's body looking perfectly preserved. Yet the coffin in the photo shows signs of rotting after six years underground.

MOUNT CARMEL CEMETERY

WHAT A voice beyond the grave

WHERE 1400 S. Wolf Rd., Hillside, IL

COST Free

PRO TIP Julia's grave is located in Section A near the Harrison Street entrance.

Left, *Known as the "Italian Bride," this memorial to Julia Buccola was commissioned after she was exhumed and her body was found in perfect condition.* Right, *According to the Italian inscription below it, this porcelain photograph was taken six years after Julia's death. Depicting soft skin and rosy cheeks identical to her wedding portrait, it was as if Julia was only sleeping.*

The Buccola family took the "incorruptible" state of Julia's body as a sign from God. They raised money to build the grand monument sculpted by Italian artists and mounted the fresh-faced photo of Julia at her exhumation on it.

Filomena's nightmares stopped, but that wasn't the last Chicagoans heard of Julia. Students from nearby Proviso West High School and drivers on Harrison Street have reported seeing a woman in white walking through the cemetery at night. Other reports claim to sense the smell of roses near her grave when there are no fresh flowers in sight. Perhaps Julia was released from the grave after all.

Julia's married name does not appear on the monument, but her mother's name is listed twice. An Italian inscription on the back reads: "Filumena Buccola I offer this Gift to My Dear Daughter Giulia."

SLEEPING GIANTS

What are those giant containers on Damen Ave.?

Chicago is the home of the skyscraper, but long before the Sears Tower was built, grain elevators stretched high above the landscape. The abandoned grain silos in Canalport serve as a reminder of Chicago's past as an agricultural powerhouse.

The thirty-five massive, gritty columns along Damen Avenue near the south branch of the Chicago River are a surprising sight nowadays. When the grain elevator was built in 1906, Chicago was a hub of transportation, industrial agriculture, and the Board of Trade's standardized wheat grading. The eighty-foot-high silos, known as the Santa Fe Railroad Grain Elevator, could store a whopping four hundred thousand bushels. Carl Sandburg's description of the city as "Stacker of Wheat" was well deserved.

The silos sat along the Illinois and Michigan Canal, which linked the Great Lakes and the Mississippi River. In 1881, boats transported more than a million tons of cargo along the canal. Nearby Canalport Riverwalk Park and Canal Origins Park pay homage to the canal's role in establishing Chicago, while providing scenic natural areas for strolling and fishing and views of the silos.

Nearby Canal Origins Park lies along the south branch of the Chicago River. It was nicknamed "Bubbly Creek" due to pollution caused by animal corpses from the Union Stockyards. The stockyards are long gone, but you may still spot bubbles in the river.

The state of Illinois's asking price for the property is $11 million.

Grain elevators have an explosive reputation. The site suffered several deadly blasts before closing for good in 1977. Now the one-hundred-year-old sentinels are silent but not forgotten. The silos serve as inspiration for adventurous urban explorers, photographers, and graffiti artists. Michael Bay featured the silos in his 2014 film *Transformers: Age of Extinction*. The Damen silos even got the documentary treatment in 2012's *Gone*, a film about a college student squatting at the silos.

Where some people see a deteriorating ruin, others see a monument to the city's legacy framing the skyline it helped build.

DAMEN SILOS

WHAT Abandoned grain elevators

WHERE 2860 S. Damen Ave.

COST Free

PRO TIP The hazardous property is owned by the state, so it's illegal to explore the Damen silos. Enjoy a safer view of the silos from Canalport Riverwalk Park.

43 WORTH ONE'S SALT

Can I rejuvenate in a cave made of salt?

If you want to reap the equivalent of three days at the seashore in forty-five minutes, head about eight miles *away* from Lake Michigan to Portage Park. There, you can soak in the healing powers of Chicago's salt caves.

Caves? Yes, Galos Caves. Although they are man-made and located in a Northwest Side strip mall, their healing abilities are not diminished. Salt caves are designed to expose people to the minerals in natural salt, which allegedly have health benefits.

The concept of salt therapy, or halotherapy, dates to medieval times, but its popularity picked up in the nineteenth century. Galos Caves installed its natural wonders in 2006 so Chicagoans could benefit from the power of salt and iodine.

For fifteen dollars a session, you can spend forty-five minutes breathing in the salty air and soaking it into your skin. After ten sessions, the caves will have you feeling as if you've returned from a month-long holiday. The salt caves claim stable air temperature and humidity as well as

In 1843, a Polish doctor noted that miners working in salt caves didn't suffer lung diseases. After World War II, Dr. Karl Hermann Spannagel started using salt therapy after noticing improvements in the health of his patients who hid in a salt cave during wartime bombings.

Crystal salt used in the caves is quite different than refined table salt on your dinner table. The salt used in Galos Caves is naturally crystallized from the Black Sea.

GALOS SALT CAVES

WHAT An unlikely maritime microclimate

WHERE 6501 W. Irving Park Rd.

COST A forty-five-minute session costs $15 for adults, $10 for seniors and students, and $8 for children ages four to twelve.

PRO TIP Bring your own white socks, or you'll be provided booties to wear in the cave.

a lack of airborne pollutants. Devotees use these visits to treat respiratory, skin, digestive, circulatory, and neurological conditions.

Upon arrival, you'll remove your shoes and enter the cave. The floor is covered with twenty pounds of imported Ukrainian salt crystals, and stalactites hang from the ceiling. You'll rest in a lounge chair nestled in fragrant salt to the sounds of New Age music. Soft colored lights and the salty aroma embrace you as you relax. Children are welcome to play with sand toys in the "salt box," but talking and electronics are forbidden.

Whether or not you become a halotherapy believer, it's a tranquil and somewhat trippy experience. Escape the city for a while and let yourself drift away to the Black Sea.

PRESIDENTIAL KISS AND TELL (page 2)

SUGAR HIGH (page 124)

CHICAGO CRAFTSMANSHIP (page 118)

EYE TO THE SKY (page 32)

SAVED FROM THE WRECKING BALL (page 62)

GROUND CONTROL (page 76)

BUTTON UP (page 26)

THE LAST PIONEER (page 178)

NO-FLY ZONE (page 74)

Be Happy

CREATIVE CONVENIENCE (page 6)

ORDINARY TOBIES
Various Colors - Graduated Sets
8.5" - 7" - 5.25" - 3.25" - 2.25" - 1.5"
Dyonmoor - 1920s

SLEEPING GIANTS (page 84)

GREEN MACHINE (page 22)

FLYING HIGH (page 10)

THE WONDERFUL PARK OF OZ (page 108)

44 THE ORIGINAL BLUES BROTHERS

Was a Rolling Stones song named after a Chicago address?

2120 South Michigan Avenue is an address so iconic that the Rolling Stones immortalized it as the title of a 1964 song. Music lovers and tourists pilgrimage here from around the world, but it's unknown to the average Chicagoan.

This South Side building was home to brothers Phil and Leonard Chess's legendary Chess Records. Chess produced hit after hit of its pioneering rhythm and blues sound in the 1950s and '60s. Chess's recordings included Etta James's "At Last," Howlin' Wolf's "Smokestack Lightning," Fontella Bass's "Rescue Me," John Lee Hooker's "One Bourbon, One Scotch, One Beer," and a teenage Aretha Franklin singing gospel. The star of Chess Records was Muddy Waters, who cut "Rollin' Stone" in 1948.

Keith Richards described reconnecting with his schoolmate Mick Jagger over Chess recordings in 1961. "You get in a carriage with a guy that's got *Rockin' at the Hops* by Chuck Berry on Chess Records, and *The Best of Muddy Waters* also under his arm, you are gonna hit it off." They took their band name from Muddy's song and recorded

In 1977, a Chess record went to outer space. The Voyager mission carried audio recordings including Chuck Berry's "Johnny B. Goode," recorded at 2120 South Michigan. If aliens like Chuck Berry, we know we're in good company.

Left, *As blues icon Buddy Guy told the Chicago Sun-Times in 2016, "[Phil and Leonard Chess] started Chess Records and made Chicago what it is today—the blues capital of the world."* Right, *The Blues Heaven Foundation seeks to preserve the music's legacy, secure royalties for blues artists, provide music education and scholarships, and offer assistance for senior blues artists. A garden named in honor of Willie Dixon is adjacent to the foundation.*

BLUES HEAVEN FOUNDATION

WHAT The epicenter of Chicago blues

WHERE 2120 S. Michigan Ave.

COST $10 per person

PRO TIP The foundation hosts a free blues concert in its garden every Wednesday night during the summer.

their first number one hit, "It's All Over Now," as well as the first version of "Satisfaction," at Chess's studio.

A key figure at Chess Records was songwriter, bassist, producer, arranger, and blues legend Willie Dixon. He wrote more than six thousand songs in his lifetime, including "I'm Your Hoochie Coochie Man" and "Little Red Rooster," which topped the charts for the Rolling Stones. A tireless advocate for the blues and its musicians, Dixon founded the Blues Heaven Foundation.

In 1997, Dixon's widow, Marie, brought the foundation home to 2120 South Michigan, saving the building from demolition. Today, you can tour a museum in the building where Koko Taylor and Bo Diddley recorded in what Richards calls "the perfect sound studio." Willie Dixon's legacy ensures that the roots of blues and rock and roll are being preserved where they started—Chicago's South Side.

45 THE WONDERFUL PARK OF OZ

Why is there a nine-foot-tall Tin Man in Lincoln Park?

You're not in Kansas anymore, but you may not believe you're in Chicago either. It's rare that literary and Hollywood heroes welcome you to their playground, but that's exactly the case at Oz Park.

This thirteen-acre space in the Lincoln Park neighborhood embraces Chicago's literary heritage. It was created in 1967 to boost revitalization back when the area didn't carry the real estate weight it does today. The park was named in 1976 to commemorate *The Wonderful Wizard of Oz* author L. Frank Baum, who wrote his famous tale while living in the city.

Sculptures of Oz characters the Tin Man, the Scarecrow, the Cowardly Lion, and Dorothy and Toto greet visitors at the park's entrances. Late Chicago sculptor John Kearney created the fanciful sculptures, financed by neighborhood donors. The kid-centric park also features a flower garden named "Emerald Garden" and a playground known as "Dorothy's Playlot." It's one of many Chicago parks that show free movies every summer, and you can bet *The Wizard of Oz* is on the bill.

Baum and illustrator W. W. Denslow visited the 1893 World's Columbian Exposition in Chicago. It's believed that Oz's Emerald City was inspired by the fair's spectacular "White City."

According to legend, Baum named his magical land after glancing at a file cabinet labeled O–Z.

OZ PARK

WHAT A storybook neighborhood hangout

WHERE Webster Ave. and Lincoln St.

COST Free

PRO TIP Follow the yellow brick road.

Despite the park's location, Baum never lived in the neighborhood. He wrote *The Wonderful Wizard of Oz* while living in Humboldt Park, a few miles west at 1667 North Humboldt Boulevard. In 2019, a developer transformed 70 feet of sidewalk in front of the address into Chicago's own yellow brick road.

When asked why he wrote fantasies, L. Frank Baum answered that he created stories for children where "wonderment and joy are retained." There's no doubt that for some Chicago children, somewhere over the rainbow is as near as their favorite park.

46

SECRET STREET

Does a hidden thoroughfare run under River North?

The Kinzie Street Bridge stands at attention on the Chicago River, fixed upright as a reminder of the city's industrial legacy. The bridge also marks the westernmost end of Carroll Avenue, a forgotten stretch of road that runs underneath some of Chicago's most prominent buildings.

Before Carroll Avenue became a subterranean secret, it was a freight route connecting Chicago businesses to the bustling Kinzie Street Bridge and the train yards beyond. The location has always been an important point of traffic. In 1832, it was the site of the first bridge built across the Chicago River, followed by the site of Chicago's first railroad bridge in 1852. For decades, Carroll Avenue carried products from the *Chicago Tribune*, *Chicago Sun-Times*, and the Curtiss Candy Company over the bridge and out to the world. The construction of the Merchandise Mart over the railroad track in 1928 made it the first place in Chicago built on air rights.

Industry eventually moved out of River North. In 2000, Carroll Avenue's last customer, the *Sun-Times*, relocated its facility. The Kinzie Street Bridge was raised and Carroll Avenue was forgotten. Or was it? Although invisible to most passersby, Carroll Avenue is still active. Businesses overhead use the underground street for deliveries and

---

The street was named after Charles Carroll, the last surviving signer of the Declaration of Independence.

Top, *This formerly prominent rail line is still used as a subterranean thoroughfare by some. Proposals in recent years have called for its redevelopment for trains or as a pedestrian street.* Bottom, *At the time of its completion in 1908, the current Kinzie Street Bridge was the longest and heaviest bascule bridge in the world. It was designated a Chicago landmark in 2007.*

CARROLL AVENUE

WHAT A subterranean lane

WHERE From the Kinzie Street Bridge east to Trump Tower

COST Free

PRO TIP Access may be limited and is blocked off in certain areas. Use common sense and caution.

garbage pickup. The corridor is home to parking garages and muddy passages. It's even known to conceal rock stars visiting the House of Blues. Their signatures are visible on the Carroll Avenue wall beneath the venue.

You can visit Carroll Avenue by looking for open service entrances along Kinzie Street, near LaSalle Street. The street is fenced off in the sections below the Apparel Center and Merchandise Mart. If you're lucky, you might catch the Kinzie Street Bridge on the one day a year it's lowered so Union Pacific can drive a truck across it to maintain its ownership.

47

HUMONGOUS HOT DOGS

What's a twelve-foot Tarzan hot dog doing in Norwood Park?

If you relish the idea of an old-fashioned drive-in, you can't miss Superdawg® on Chicago's Northwest Side. That's because two twelve-foot hot dogs with glowing red eyes beckon you from the restaurant's roof!

Maurie sports a Tarzan tunic and a strongman pose, while Flaurie winks at him wearing a blue bow and skirt. They are the mascots of Superdawg's founders, Maurice and Florence Berman, who started the restaurant in 1948. After Maurie returned from World War II, he and his high school sweetheart, Florence, opened a roadside hot dog stand at the corner of Milwaukee, Devon, and Nagle Streets.

While hot dog shops were popping up all over the country, the Bermans were determined to stand out. They gave their restaurant a distinctive name inspired by the new superhero comics of the 1940s. Maurie designed the building topped with its iconic wieners beckoning hungry visitors. He also designed the glowing blue control tower where carhops take orders from a switchboard. But what really sets Superdawg apart is its secret recipe, created by Maurie and Flaurie.

SUPERDAWG® DRIVE-IN

WHAT A Chicago-style drive-in

WHERE 6363 N. Milwaukee Ave. There is a second location in Wheeling, IL.

COST For $5.90 you'll get a pure beef Superdawg on a poppy seed bun with all the trimmings and a side of Superfries™.

PRO TIP Join the Superdining Club newsletter to receive a free treat on your birthday and anniversary.

Superdawg may be responsible for the mustard on your hot dog emoji. In 2014, they started a campaign to get the American food favorite added to Unicode. Although not Chicago-style, a hot dog emoji was added the following year.

Today, you can still get the same classic Superdawg experience. The restaurant is owned and operated by the children and grandchildren of Maurice and Florence. Visitors pull into the drive-in and order a Whoopskidawg®, Whoopercheesie®, or Supermalt® through the intercom. A carhop rests your Superdawg nestled on a bed of crinkle fries in a signature box on a tray that hooks onto your window. Relax in your ride and enjoy your Chicago-style treat, then flip the switch to let the carport know when you're finished.

Each visit is rewarded with Superdawg's signature sendoff, "HIYA!! . . . From the bottom of our pure beef hearts, thanks for stopping."

Spot Superdawg trays in the 1984 John Hughes film *Sixteen Candles*, which was set and shot in Chicago.

48

CLASSIFIED SUPPLIES

Where can an agent on the go find a good fake mustache these days?

You're on a mission. The target is in sight, but you've run out of invisible ink. Fortunately, there's a rendezvous point at the Wicker Park Secret Agent Supply Co.

The shop specializes in all things espionage, from rearview spy glasses to false bottom soda cans for hiding classified items. There are plenty of writing supplies for crafting your vital messages. There's also an extensive book collection, including anthologies written by Chicago students.

The supply shop has a secret of its own. It's harboring a 3,200-square-foot creative writing and tutoring center called 826CHI. It's the Chicago chapter of 826 National, a nonprofit organization founded by author Dave Eggers. Every chapter has a themed storefront ranging from a robot factory to a pirate supply shop.

Since 2005, 826CHI has provided free support to students ages six to eighteen, with an emphasis on creative and expository writing skills. The center hosts writing workshops, one-on-one tutoring sessions, and field trips. It prints student writing in its publishing center and then sells the finished products in the store. Students and authors can read their work to the community from a small stage. They serve about 2,500 students from more than one hundred different schools each year!

Check out the store's Facebook page for information on upcoming public events including readings, workshops, craft fairs, panel discussions, and live music.

Agents of any age will enjoy the unique gift selection at the Wicker Park Secret Agent Supply Co.

"The store is designed to bring people in and educate the community about what we do," says operations manager Tyler Stoltenberg. "Seeing the secret door that leads to our tutoring center blows people's minds."

Along with spy gear, the Secret Agent Supply Co. stocks items that align with 826CHI's mission—inspiring imagination and promoting diversity and social justice. Its best-selling items include student publications and invisible ink pens. Every purchase supports 826CHI's free programs. So the next time you're in the market for a diving bell mask or just some creative inspiration, stop by the Secret Agent Supply Co. and support the next generation of Chicago writers.

WICKER PARK SECRET AGENT SUPPLY CO.

WHAT A spy store with a not-so-secret mission

WHERE 1276 N. Milwaukee Ave.

COST Items range from $1 to $50.

PRO TIP The tutoring center's library is stored on Morse code bookshelves. Can you decode its message?

49 DANCE-FLOOR DIPLOMACY

Where can I find Chicago's most inclusive dance party?

In a city as large as Chicago, you expect to encounter a fabric of countless subcultures and communities. Yet it's rare to find them all in one place. If you're looking for an intersectional space featuring the city's up-and-coming artistic talent, Stardust delivers dance-floor diplomacy for all Chicagoans.

Every Thursday night, Stardust parties showcase a collaboration of emerging artists, performers, DJs, fashion designers, and club personalities at Berlin Nightclub. These events happen under one of many aliases that strive to be a platform for celebrating the art and awareness of underrepresented communities including queer, trans, femme, minority, and nonbinary performers.

Diversity has been essential to Berlin's DNA since its beginning in 1983. "It was about creating a safe space for those who just didn't fit in a mold," co-owner Jo Webster told the *Chicago Tribune* in 2013. A typical night might include goths, drag queens, and queer and straight music fans getting down on the dance floor together.

Stardust parties in particular have a cultural cachet as supportive and innovative spaces among underrepresented

---

As part of their mission to create safer, braver spaces in nightlife, art collective and Stardust collaborators IT Presents created a zine in 2016. The IT Zine for Brave Spaces offers thoughts, coping mechanisms, and resources for navigating nightlife.

Gavin Rayna Russom played her first gig after coming out as transgender at Femme's Room, a party celebrating femininity and femme expression. "There was such a broad spectrum of humanity expressing themselves in that room," she says. "It made me so joyful."

BERLIN NIGHTCLUB

WHAT An inclusive slice of nightlife

WHERE 954 W. Belmont Ave.

COST $10 cover

NOTEWORTHY Berlin's bathrooms have always been gender neutral. In 2011, it was the first to identify as a trans-friendly business in the Chicago T-Friendly Bathroom Initiative.

performance communities. In 2017, musician and LCD Soundsystem band member Gavin Rayna Russom gave her first performance after coming out as transgender at Stardust's Femme's Room. "To have a space that's not only queer and trans affirming but also explicitly femme affirming is so important," she says. "I'm just grateful that it exists and that I got to play there."

On any given Thursday at Berlin, you can expect an out-of-the-box experience from Stardust. "The goal is to keep being progressive," says Stardust promoter Scott Cramer. "We want to be as intersectional as possible using our events as a medium." However you identify, once you're in on the Stardust secret, you'll keep coming back. As Russom says, "By sharing space and conversation and music with each other, we can all help each other figure ourselves out."

50

CHICAGO CRAFTSMANSHIP

Is the work of a modern Renaissance man hidden in Old Town?

Chicago rings with the names of architectural icons like Frank Lloyd Wright, Louis Sullivan, and Ludwig Mies van der Rohe. Yet one of the city's most multitalented and prolific artists is virtually unknown today. Edgar Miller's work is hiding throughout the city, particularly on the quiet streets of Old Town.

Walking through the neighborhood on North Wells Street, you may have noticed an area where the blocks of brick are broken up by the appearance of colorful tiles. This is a mere hint of the flights of fancy and feats of craftsmanship inside the R. W. Glasner Studio. The home is one of four that Miller and his business partner Sol Kogen converted into artists' flats in the 1920s and '30s.

Largely self-taught, Miller worked in about thirty mediums! Not only did he design his work, he executed it. Examples of his painting, sculpture, stained glass, wood carving, iron working, and printmaking adorn Glasner Studio. The interior is a riotous symphony of styles. Hand-carved medieval animals parade by while stained glass representations of love look on. Every surface is carved, painted, and packed with symbolism.

One reason history overlooks Miller is that he's impossible to categorize, drawing influence from Arts and Crafts, Art Deco, Native American motifs, and

R. W. GLASNER STUDIO

WHAT An artist's imagination come to life

WHERE 1734 N. Wells St.

COST $25

PRO TIP The studio is part of a private residential complex, so tours are restricted to the second Saturday of every month, September through May.

Miller's work emphasizes animals and nature. "I indulged my enjoyment of animals—animals in action—all different kinds of animals," he said. "The incredible richness of the earth is to blame for all of these plants and animals."

frontier folk art. Miller pioneered the use of reclaimed materials decades before it was in vogue. He recycled old bathroom tiles into roofing and used industrial glass in mosaics. Reflecting on his work, Miller said, "I accepted influences from any place."

Miller gained notoriety in his day. In 1932, *Architecture* magazine declared that "a new luminary has risen in American decorative art. Each fresh product of Edgar Miller, designer-craftsman, of Chicago, is proof of this." His genius is now overlooked because his work lives on in private, "handmade homes," not museums. Fortunately, his visionary spaces are hidden in plain sight.

You can see Miller's work elsewhere in town, including at the Standard Club, Kelvyn Park High School, the Trustees System Service Building, and King Arthur Court at the InterContinental Chicago.

51

ALPHABET TOWN

Are Chicago's streets alphabetized?

If you're heading west from Pulaski Road, you might notice a pattern developing among the street signs. Karlov, Kedvale, Keeler—the K-named streets stretch on for a mile. This isn't a coincidence; it's a clever bit of urban planning that is often overlooked.

In the early twentieth century, Chicago's residential development was quickly growing outside the Loop. The north–south streets west of Pulaski Road were numbered by their distance from State Street, as are most of the city's streets. To avoid the confusion of seeing a 35th Street on both the South Side and the West Side, they renamed the western streets with words.

In 1913, Chicago's planning commission approved a new street-naming system to rename north–south streets. The system assigned a letter every mile starting from "A" at the first mile west of the Indiana border. The city council resisted renaming roads that had established names, like Michigan Avenue, and began the alphabetical naming convention with newer streets west of Pulaski Road.

This is why you'll see Kostner, Kenneth, and Kilbourn Avenues follow each other. Locals have nicknamed the area "K-Town." When you reach the next mile marker, the

---

Another alphabet soup of street names can be found in Hegewisch on Chicago's Southeast Side. A handful of north–south streets run from Avenue A west to Avenue O.

When you've entered the "K" streets, you know you're eleven miles west of the Indiana border.

ALPHABET TOWN

WHAT A wordy street-naming convention

WHERE Streets from Pulaski Street west to the edge of Chicago

COST Free

NOTEWORTHY Brennan Avenue is named in honor of Edward Brennan, the city council member who championed the citywide street-numbering system.

streets begin with the letter "L" at Lavergne and Lawler. This alphabetical pattern continues through P, where Chicago's city limit meets Norridge and Elmwood Park.

Old Irving Park, however, is missing several "K" streets. The neighborhood was developed as a subdivision in the late nineteenth century with lots twice as large as Chicago's standard. To enlarge the lots, some streets had to go. See ya later, Komesky, Kolin, and Karlov Streets.

So the next time you find yourself at Mango Street, you'll know that you're thirteen miles from the Indiana border. Here's hoping that Chicago will continue to grow so we can see what creative "Q-Town" streets are christened west of O'Hare.

52

ROCK ON

How did all those famous stones get embedded in the Tribune Tower?

The Tribune Tower is one of Chicago's most iconic buildings. After all, its neo-Gothic design won a 1922 competition for "the most beautiful office building in the world." Yet one of the most curious features of the building's facade was nowhere in the original plans—the collection of stones from around the world.

It's not hard to spot the 150 fragments of famous sites from all over the world embedded in the skyscraper's Indiana limestone walls. The stones include sites from all fifty states, the Great Wall of China, the Berlin Wall, and the Great Pyramid at Cheops. Exploring the exterior is like a quick trip around the world for observant tourists and curious Chicagoans. But how did a piece of the Taj Mahal end up on Michigan Avenue?

The collection started in 1915 when *Chicago Tribune* publisher Robert R. McCormick traveled to Europe covering World War I. Upon visiting the ruins of a medieval Belgian cathedral at Ypres, McCormick took a piece of rubble from the site.

After the Tribune Tower design competition, "The Colonel," as McCormick was known, wanted to decorate

Witty sculptures called grotesques cover the building to express the ideals of journalism. Look above the main entrance for a whispering man and a shouting man, who symbolize the difference between rumor and a hot story.

This piece of the Great Pyramid is one of 150 fragments from famous locations around the world embedded in the Tribune Tower's exterior.

TRIBUNE TOWER

WHAT An impressive rock collection

WHERE 435 N. Michigan Ave.

COST Free

PRO TIP Step inside to admire the grand lobby, including an enormous relief map of the United States made from retired US currency.

its outside walls. He instructed his correspondents to procure "stones about six inches square from such buildings as the Law Courts of Dublin, the Parthenon at Athens, St. Sophia Cathedral, or any other famous cathedral or palace or ruin." Fragments were to be gathered "by honorable means," but some pieces were acquired covertly, like a Kremlin brick smuggled by a Finnish diplomat in 1933.

McCormick hoped that associating the *Chicago Tribune* with the world's greatest buildings would advance the standing of the newspaper and city. Per architecture critic Blair Kamin, "Far from being a mere curiosity, however, these bits and pieces of history speak volumes about the oversized aspirations of Tribune Tower's creators: to make their fledgling skyscraper one of the world's great monuments."

53 SUGAR HIGH

Where can I find the largest selection of Mexican candy in the Midwest?

You might guess that Michigan Avenue is Chicago's highest-grossing shopping thoroughfare. However, you probably didn't know that the city's second busiest commercial district is in Little Village. La Villita, as it's known locally, is nicknamed the "Mexico of the Midwest." Among the businesses on 26th Street's vibrant corridor is a candyland fit to satisfy any sweet tooth.

Dulcelandia means "candyland" in English, and this store has been giving Willy Wonka a run for his money since 1995. What's that sweet aroma that hits you upon entering the store? The smell of the largest Mexican candy distributor in the Midwest. The family-run business stocks a dizzying selection of more than six hundred varieties of Mexican and American sweets displayed on shelves, piled high in bins, and arranged in decorative towers.

These are confectionary flavors you won't find elsewhere in Chicago, like tamarind, mango, guava, and pollito asado, or spicy peach lollipops in the shape of roasted chickens.

About five hundred businesses line the two-mile stretch of 26th Street between Kedzie and Kostner Avenues in Little Village, where you can buy everything from cowboy hats to pushcart *elotes*. According to *Crain's Chicago Business,* around five hundred thousand Mexican Americans live within a ten-minute drive of the shopping district.

Sugar junkies visit to enjoy a nostalgic taste of their favorite candies from childhood. Guests have traveled from as far as France to sample Dulcelandia's incredible selection.

DULCELANDIA

WHAT South of the border sweets

WHERE 3253 W. 26th St.

COST Candy ranges from ten cents to $8 per pound; piñatas range from $9.99 to $34.99.

PRO TIP Dulcelandia also has locations in Chicago's Brighton Park and Logan Square neighborhoods.

Dulcelandia allows you to buy in bulk so you can get your sweet on without breaking the bank.

While the walls are bursting with candy, Dulcelandia's ceilings are decked in piñatas. Lively figures and colorful streamers dangle overhead, completing the party atmosphere. The shop is the Midwest's largest provider of piñatas, also imported from Mexico.

Feeling like frozen yogurt? The city's most distinctive varieties are inside at Yogolandia. Exclusive flavors like horchata, flan, and chocolate abuelita have a Mexican flair. Top your sweet treat with traditional fixings like gummy worms or Little Village–inspired toppings like churros and marzipan.

Dulcelandia's walls feature traditional Mexican murals of ancient Mayans creating chocolate and people breaking piñatas. Today's shoppers can take comfort knowing we're only the latest in a long line of sweet freaks.

54

A LEAGUE OF THEIR OWN

Where do Cubs fans rest in peace?

Cubs fans waited a lifetime to see their team win a World Series in 2016. Yet for some, one lifetime isn't long enough to cheer on the North Side team. At the Bohemian National Cemetery, diehard fans can pledge their immortal baseball loyalty by being laid to rest in a Wrigley Field replica.

The Northwest Side cemetery is home to a slice of Wrigleyville, despite being five miles away.

"Beyond the Vines" is a columbarium, or burial wall, containing the remains of eternal Cubs fans in cremation urns. Ivy climbs the twenty-four-foot-long red brick center field wall, which features a yellow four-hundred-foot marker. A stained glass scoreboard is perpetually set to 1:20 p.m., the start time of the home opener. Visitors can rest on a bullpen bench or stadium seats direct from Wrigley Field. A home plate, turf, dirt around the wall, and paver stones all from the ballpark complete the scene. The cemetery stopped short of broadcasting live Cubs games.

The wall was dedicated in 2009, after Dennis Mascari purchased the property, funded the wall, and donated it to the cemetery. His goal was to make cemetery visits more enjoyable, another kind of friendly confines. Mascari was

---

The cemetery features a memorial to victims of the 1915 Eastland Disaster. About 150 victims of the disaster were laid to rest here, the highest number of victims' bodies buried at any Chicago cemetery.

Left, *If Wrigley Field is your second home in this life, Beyond the Vines may be the ideal place for your afterlife.* Right, *Visitors to Beyond the Vines leave mementos like ticket stubs and baseball cards for their loved ones.*

buried here himself in 2011, occupying one of the 288 burial niches.

So how do you reserve a spot in one of the "eternal sky boxes"? Spaces start at around sixteen hundred dollars. As Harry Caray would say, "Holy cow!" Those who prefer gravesites can rest nearby, in coffins featuring the Cubs logo, of course.

A "W" flies above the cemetery gate at this Northwest Side resting place. While many residents never lived to see the Cubbies take home the championship, these true-blue Cubs fans will be ready to play two for eternity.

BOHEMIAN NATIONAL CEMETERY

WHAT A final resting place for super fans

WHERE 5255 N. Pulaski Rd.

COST Free

NOTEWORTHY Czech Chicago mayor Anton Cermak is the cemetery's most famous resident.

55

JUGHEADS

How can I see eight thousand colorful faces at once?

A good collection can make the past come alive and forge connections with characters of all kinds. Evanston resident Stephen Mullins began collecting character jugs in 1947. His collection of Toby jugs grew from the first six he bought at summer camp to the world's largest. You can see more than eight thousand Toby and character jugs at Mullins's museum in Evanston.

So, what is a Toby jug, anyway? It's a ceramic pitcher shaped like a historic or fictional character. Back in 1760s England, the first Toby jugs depicted a seated man holding a pipe and a mug of ale. They wore a tricorn hat, which formed a pouring spout, and were common vessels at taverns. Toby jugs portray a subject's full body, while character jugs only include the head and shoulders. Since then, Toby jugs have humorously depicted everyone from US presidents to *Star Wars* characters. Some even have music boxes attached to them!

No one is quite sure how these charming vessels came to be called "Tobies." They may refer to the character of Sir Toby Belch in *Twelfth Night*. Another legend attributes the name to a heavy Yorkshire drinker nicknamed "Toby Fillpot," as inspired by the old drinking song "The Brown Jug."

Hidden behind an inconspicuous street-level entrance, the American Toby Jug Museum features ceramics from

---

Don't confuse jugs with mugs. While mugs are used for drinking, jugs are used for pouring and have a spout on their rim.

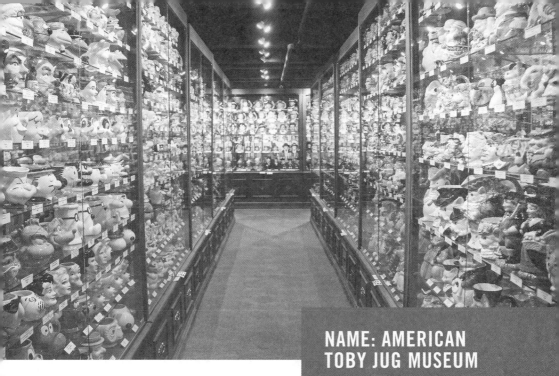

Virtually every figure from history and pop culture is depicted in the world's largest collection of Toby and character jugs! The eight-thousand-piece collection includes characters from Shakespeare to Looney Tunes.

NAME: AMERICAN TOBY JUG MUSEUM

WHAT Pitchers with personality

WHERE 910 Chicago Ave., Evanston, IL

COST Free

PRO TIP Sneak a peek! The shelves are mirrored so you can see the craftsmanship of each Toby's handle.

more than two hundred makers and thirty different countries. Ceramic faces smile from the one hundred cabinets in the museum, arranged by age, manufacturer, and category. The characters represented in the collection speak to its range from the 1760s through work still in production by three companies today. The museum has even commissioned jugs, including a series of World War II Allied leaders.

Toby jugs are a fun representation of culture and craftsmanship. It's fascinating to walk through the museum and watch history unfold across the world as characters of each generation come to life in this unique art form.

56

UNDERGROUND CHINATOWN

Are some of Chinatown's best eats hiding in a basement food court?

Chicago's Chinatown is a hub of cuisine. Whether you're hungry for BBQ, bakeries, simmering hot pot, or spicy Szechuan, there's a restaurant to satisfy every craving. Some of Chinatown's best food isn't found on Wentworth Avenue, however, but *under* it.

Skip the trendy restaurant lines and head for Richland Center, a mall at the northeast edge of Chinatown Square. Like any good mall, Richland Center has a food court, and this one is underground. Descend to the basement to score cheap and easy eats.

The fluorescent-lit cafeteria is no match for some of the eye-catching ambiance above ground, but its ten stalls deliver on taste. Each walk-up stall offers different food items. You can find everything from chicken feet to Szechuan duck neck and from stir-fry to noodle soup.

Taiwanese snack shop Hello Jasmine deals in bubble teas and mouthwatering chicken-fried steak strips. Tientsin Potstickers delivers crispy dumplings in varieties like lamb cilantro. You can even taste Japanese offerings at Ike Bukuro Sushi and Ky Lin Teppanyaki.

Fair warning that your favorite stall on one visit may be replaced by a new restaurant on your next trip.

RICHLAND CENTER FOOD COURT

WHAT Subterranean Chinese eats

WHERE 2002 S. Wentworth Ave.

COST Starting at $5

PRO TIP Need a salon, acupuncturist, or rice cooker? You'll find them downstairs.

This Chinatown food court serves as an incubator for new restaurants to launch. Until about 1910, Chicago's first Chinatown was located in the Loop on Clark Street between Van Buren and Harrison.

The stalls serve as a low-cost way for new restaurants to launch. As the mall's developer told the *Chicago Reader* in 2010, "A lot of little entrepreneurs I come across don't have enough revenue to start a full-fledged restaurant. But here it is much cheaper for them to run." By eating at the Richland Center food court, you're often getting the first taste of Chinatown's newest dishes.

Nearby, Qing Xiang Yuan Dumpling is one of the restaurant incubator's success stories. It started out as a soup dumpling stall in the food court before growing into its own full-service space.

The food court's variety and value make it a great place to experiment with new cuisines. Try a dish from each stall, and support Chicago's entrepreneurs while expanding your palate!

A little-known museum is located just down the street. The Dr. Sun Yat-Sen Museum of Chicago celebrates the medical doctor who became the "Father of the Chinese Revolution."

57

LIGHTS, CAMERA, ACTION!

Is this Victorian house home to a legendary film company?

This two-story house blends into its Lakeview neighborhood, but to independent filmmakers it's a sacred space. It's home to Kartemquin Films, the powerhouse documentary production company that's sparked social commentary through film for more than fifty years.

The nonprofit collective was founded in 1966 by three University of Chicago graduates. Stan Karter, Jerry Temaner, and Gordon Quinn combined their names to create Kartemquin Films. Their mission was to create documentaries focusing on people whose lives are directly affected by social and political change and who are often overlooked or misrepresented by the media.

Kartemquin began as a collective of filmmakers, activists, teachers, students, and social workers working for "cinematic social inquiry." In 1971, they purchased the former dry-cleaning business in a mixed, working-class area for only $21,500. "We thought moving into a neighborhood would make a difference," says founding member Gordon Quinn. "We wanted to connect to the working class." Soon enough, the local union was holding elections in their basement and using their kitchen to feed striking workers.

Kartemquin's name was also created to rhyme with the classic 1925 Sergei Eisenstein film *Battleship Potemkin* as an homage. Cofounder Jerry Blumenthal's name was not added to the portmanteau.

Kartemquin's first film was Home for Life *(1966), featuring people entering a home for the aged. Other works have highlighted labor struggles, homelessness, and immigration. Kartemquin's best-known film,* Hoop Dreams *(1994), was, at that time, the highest-grossing documentary ever produced. Recent works include* The Interrupters *(2011) and* Life Itself *(2014), a Roger Ebert biopic.*

KARTEMQUIN FILMS

WHAT Democracy through documentary

WHERE 1901 W. Wellington Ave.

COST Free

PRO TIP Check www.kartemquin.com for the latest events and screenings.

Today, the house is still buzzing with about fifteen documentary projects at any given time, as well as an internship program and archival work. Film posters and awards line the walls while shelves are crammed with tapes, hard drives, and equipment. "It's not about the furniture or the paint on the walls; this is a place to be creative, and our resources go toward telling stories," says Quinn.

Kartemquin's programming goes beyond producing films. They run community programs including the Diverse Voices in Docs mentorship program for minority filmmakers and KTQ Labs, which provides filmmakers with free critiques. Kartemquin is a testament to five decades of collaboration on social justice. According to Chaz Ebert, widow of Roger, "These are not just films. They are capsules of humanity that touch hearts and change minds."

58

THE DRIFTER

Where can I watch a burlesque show in an authentic Chicago speakeasy?

Plenty of Chicago watering holes tout the city's sudsy past, but River North is home to one authentic Prohibition-era bar with a secret act downstairs.

The Green Door Tavern is a classic Chicago saloon. The two-story balloon frame wooden structure was built in 1872, one year after a certain fire put wooden buildings out of fashion. Chicago soon outlawed the construction of wooden commercial buildings in the central business district, making this remaining building a rarity. It began as a grocery store and then turned into a restaurant, eventually becoming known as the Green Door.

The Green Door bills itself as "Chicago's oldest tavern." Its name refers to the Prohibition-era practice of painting a door green to indicate the presence of a speakeasy. It denoted that you paid the proper authorities "the green" to keep operating. The six-foot-tall illuminated sign on the tavern's roof isn't hiding anything, but what's downstairs might surprise you.

Head toward the restrooms and keep an eye out for a tchotchke cabinet. What looks like a solid wall is actually

---

If you feel the building leaning, your beers might not be to blame. The building began leaning shortly after it settled. The Green Door's famous tilt has been disorienting drinkers for nearly 150 years!

Left, *A soapbox derby car, jackalope, vintage wooden icebox, and antique cash register are just a few of the items to drink in at the Green Door.* Right, *After decades as a storage space, the basement is a saloon once more. The antique bottles displayed near the bar were all found in the space. During renovation, the owners also uncovered a secret door that Prohibition-era imbibers used for transporting booze.*

THE DRIFTER

WHAT A modern speakeasy in a Prohibition-era tavern

WHERE 678 N. Orleans St.

COST Cocktails at the Drifter are $12.

PRO TIP Adventurous patrons opt for a drink from the shot wheel.

the entrance to the Drifter, a modern speakeasy in a Prohibition basement. The original bar and wall hangings remain from the space's time as a speakeasy on gangster Dean O'Banion's circuit.

The tiny lounge seats forty people in a sideshow jewel box draped in circus tapestries. Select a cocktail from the list printed on tarot cards and enjoy the night's entertainment. As you take in the burlesque, magic, or sword-swallowing acts, you feel a world away from the streets above.

The Green Door has watched the surrounding neighborhood change from the industrial Smokey Hollow one hundred years ago to the trendy high-rise mecca it is today. As a sign in the bar proclaims, "You are now entering another era. Enjoy it now."

59

THE MOST BEAUTIFUL CHURCH IN AMERICA

Is Chicago home to the country's most beautiful church?

Many Chicagoans recognize the 130-foot tower of St. John Cantius Church from driving past on the Kennedy Expressway. How many would guess that the building is home to the most beautiful church in the United States?

In 2016, St. John Cantius took top honors in a contest called Church Madness. The *Art and Liturgy* blog ran a bracket-style challenge highlighting sixty-four architecturally significant houses of worship across the United States. After sixteen thousand votes were cast, St. John Cantius was named the most beautiful church in America.

Founded by Polish immigrants, the church took five years to build and was completed in 1898. It's baroque interior, including elaborately carved woodwork, resembles the opulent art of eighteenth-century Kraków.

ST. JOHN CANTIUS CHURCH

WHAT A stunning sanctuary

WHERE 825 N. Carpenter St.

COST Free

NOTEWORTHY The church is known for its program of solemn liturgies and devotions and rich music like Gregorian chants and classical compositions.

This magnificent sacred space has inspired Chicagoans for more than a century.

At its height around 1918, the parish had 23,000 parishioners and 2,500 children in the school. The congregation scattered after the Great Depression, and the church was slated for closure. Fortunately, the church survived and the interior was restored in 2012.

St. John Cantius is located in River West, which was once known as "Expatriate Poland" or the "Polish Patch." It's one of several "Polish Cathedral" churches in Chicago.

The church contains several unexpected treasures. After you're dazzled by the ornate main altar and two side altars dating from the 1893 World's Columbian Exposition, head for the chapel. Inside, a cabinet opens to reveal a glorious carved gold picture book of sorts. The intricate carving is a one-third scale replica of the Veit Stoss Altar of St. Mary's Basilica in Kraków. It took artist Michał Batkiewicz eight years to complete!

The church also hosts a permanent exhibit of sacred art in the north tower. Visit on Sundays to see an exquisite Neapolitan crèche, a nineteenth-century pietà from Bavaria, and hundreds of authenticated relics of saints.

There's no denying the beauty of St. John Cantius, which has stood in Chicago for more than one hundred years. Like the city itself, it's a true Renaissance story.

St. John Cantius's treasures include a nineteenth-century copy of Our Lady of Częstochowa. The jeweled crowns adorning Mary and Jesus were made from jewelry donated by parishioners. It was blessed by Pope John Paul II, who declared it "Our Lady of Chicago."

137

60

FOLLOW THE WOODEN BLOCK ROAD

Where can you find a Chicago street paved in wood?

It's nice to have a few constants to rely on in an ever-changing city. In Chicago, these include complaints about the winters, crooked politicians, and pothole-ridden roads. Yet there was a time when the city was paved not with asphalt or stones, but with wood. Chicago's wooden streets have disappeared, but you can still walk upon the past in a few wooden alleys.

In the 1850s, Chicago lumber was cheap thanks to Wisconsin's nearby forests. The city began experimenting with a wood block pavement known as Nicholson pavement. Chicago's civil engineer, Samuel Greeley, praised this wooden pavement "where lumber was the great staple of the market, and where the foundation was new and yielding."

Wood block pavement promised to be durable, clean, and quiet. The pavement was constructed from four-inch-wide, twelve-inch-long wooden blocks. The blocks settled on a sand foundation filled with gravel and coal tar to keep out moisture. When pine blocks proved to wear out quickly, the city switched to the more durable white oak and cedar.

The durable wood pavement even survived the Great Chicago Fire! An 1872 report stated, "The wooden block pavement, although considerably damaged on all the streets where it was laid, withstood the fire much better than was expected."

WOOD BLOCK ALLEY

WHAT A preserved bit of blockheaded infrastructure

WHERE Alley between North State Pkwy. and North Astor St.

COST Free

PRO TIP The alley is located behind the archbishop of Chicago's residence.

Top, *This wood block alley was built in 1909 at a cost of $3,346.96. It was placed on the National Register in 2002 and restored in 2011 at a cost of $400,000.* Bottom, *In 2016, a road crew in Auburn Gresham uncovered a century-old wood-paved street. According to the Chicago History Museum, there are miles of wooden paving remaining under the city streets that were simply paved over.*

By 1891, 62 percent of Chicago's 774 miles of road were paved with wood.

Still, the life of a wood block was only about a decade. Wood block pavement fell out of favor by the turn of the century as wood resources were depleted and stone became more affordable.

You can still stumble on crumbling wood block alleys around 2100 North Hudson south of Webster Avenue and on Roscoe Street west of the Inner Drive. Chicago's best-known wood block alley lies in the Gold Coast between State Parkway and Astor Street. Residents and aldermen restored the historic wood block alley in 2011, using both original and new blocks. The alley now boasts black locust pavers set in sand with concrete bands. It's a fitting tribute to the forgotten building blocks that helped the city boom.

61

BIG SHOES TO FILL

Where are those enormous leg sculptures in Grant Park headed?

Countless people walk by Grant Park each day, mimicking a massive public artwork at its south end. The group of 106 sculptures stands nine feet high, poised in motion. What do these headless giants represent and where are they going?

The sculptures began their walk in the park in 2006, when they were installed by internationally acclaimed artist Magdalena Abakanowicz. The Polish sculptor and three assistants created the model for each figure by hand. They were cast in a foundry in Poznań over a two-year period before being transported to the United States. Just as nature never repeats itself, no two pieces are alike.

The artwork's name, *Agora*, refers to a central meeting place in ancient Greece. The sculptures congregate in Grant Park, yet they are all facing different directions. The sturdy, rust-colored figures have a textured exterior that's veined like old-growth trees. They stretch upward from their toes until they're cut off above the torso. Their cast-iron frames seem frozen in time against the city skyline.

Visitors can walk through the pieces and engage with the artwork from many different angles. There's no consensus on whether *Agora* is eerie or inspiring. Some find the artwork to be cold and anxious. Others believe the work represents democracy and the power of the independent mind.

Agora was valued at $10 million at its installation.

Even without a head or arms, each cast-iron figure weighs 1,800 pounds.

AGORA

WHAT Public art that walks the walk

WHERE Roosevelt Rd. and Michigan Ave.

COST Free

PRO TIP Walk through the sculptures to appreciate the work from different angles.

"People who are frightened of this piece or think it should be beautiful would like to have it explained to the very end," Abakanowicz told the *Chicago Tribune* in 2006. "But the piece is about many different problems we feel and don't want to speak about."

Chicago has long been home to figures that march to a different beat, and these sculptures are no exception.

62

ON YOUR MARK

How did a British-style village end up in industrial East Chicago?

Just outside Chicago, three miles east of the Illinois border, there's a quaint British village. It's an unlikely location, with the pastel bungalows nestled among the plumage of nearby steel mills and oil refineries. The neighborhood of Marktown has persevered for a century, but its unique identity is under threat.

The industrial community was built in 1917 as a model factory town. Industrialist Clayton Mark hoped to ensure a loyal workforce at his adjacent steel mill by providing them a utopian community. Employees who stayed on the job for five years received a discount on purchasing Marktown homes. He planned to house more than eight thousand Indiana Harbor Works employees at the site and cover twenty acres of land. Due to the effects of World War I, only 10 percent of the planned community was built, and Mark sold his company in 1923.

Noted architect Howard Van Doren Shaw designed the model town according to the Garden City concept of the era. Although it's surrounded by factories on three sides, Marktown was meant to invoke an English village. About two hundred colorful Tudor-style homes cluster along narrow lanes. The streets are so slender that residents park their cars on the sidewalks and walk in the road.

The closeness of the buildings reflects the closeness of Marktown's tight-knit community. Many families have lived

MARKTOWN

WHAT A bit of Britain in Chicagoland

WHERE 405 Prospect St., East Chicago, IN

COST Free

PRO TIP A historic driving tour and walking tour can be found at www.marktown.org.

Left, Similar to some European towns, Marktown's narrow streets require residents to park on the sidewalk and walk in the road. This practice earned the community a mention in Ripley's Believe It or Not! *Right, Marktown was added to the National Register of Historic Places in 1975, but this hasn't prevented BP from purchasing and demolishing homes around its nearby Whiting Refinery.*

here for generations. However, the neighborhood shows signs of deterioration as its population dwindles. Fifty Marktown properties have been bought, and in some cases demolished, by BP. Marktown celebrated its centennial in 2017. Here's hoping this unique community is preserved to see its next one hundred years.

Chicago's other British-inspired neighborhood is located a block north of Wrigley Field. Alta Vista Terrace is a residential neighborhood designed to resemble a street of London townhomes. The forty homes were built in 1904 in a range of architectural styles, and each house has a twin diagonally across the street from it.

63

OTHERWORLDLY READS

Where can I learn to communicate with the spirit world?

The word *occult* means "hidden" or "beyond the realm of human comprehension," and one shop in Noble Square is especially equipped to help you address life's mysteries. Founded in 1918, the Occult Bookstore bills itself as the oldest spiritual shop in the world.

D. G. Nelson established the store to dedicate a space to serve as a mystical resource and spiritual institution. Nelson was an astrologer and face reader who gained notoriety reading faces in the Loop. The shop began at 611 North State Street, where many occult world personalities visited, and spent time at Clark and Belmont before settling on Milwaukee Avenue in 2006. One hundred years later, the Occult Bookstore continues to supply esoteric texts and materials with a commitment to fostering the spiritual community.

Entering an occult store may sound intimidating, but a unicorn in the window welcomes visitors inside. Shelves are filled with a wide range of books on topics from spiritual doctrine to psychology and homeopathy. Read up on demons or astrology as incense burns and music plays

---

The Occult Bookstore runs a community garden. Volunteers meet to tend the garden and learn about corresponding elements and their planetary associations. Magical plants grown here are later used in the store.

From portable magic to divination, the Occult Bookstore has all your alternative spirituality needs covered.

THE OCCULT BOOKSTORE

WHAT The world's oldest spiritual shop

WHERE 1164 N. Milwaukee Ave.

COST Pick up a natural rose quartz for $2 or an ancient fire opal ammonite for $300.

PRO TIP Photos are prohibited inside the store.

gently in the background. Tapestries, art, and live altars line the walls. Patrons browse the crystals and potions, and the enthusiastic staff is always happy to provide guidance. It's a reflective environment for exploring the shop's eclectic contents.

The staff represents a pan-traditional team of spiritual practitioners with expertise in everything from angelic magic to ancient Sumerian rites. The store also hosts weekly workshops and community discussions on themes like metaphysics. Learn to cure your lovesickness or ward off alien attacks. You don't need to be an aspiring shaman to visit the Occult Bookstore; you just need to have a mind open to the possibilities of the universe.

Where can I sunbathe on a Lake Michigan shipwreck?

You can see a lot of interesting things from the Lakefront Trail, Chicago's eighteen-mile paved path along the Lake Michigan shoreline. Around 49th Street, you'll notice birds or swimmers sunning on a rock about two hundred yards from shore. Only that's not a rock poking above the lake's surface—it's part of a shipwreck.

That object is actually the rusty remains of a ship's boiler. On July 15, 1914, a 109-foot steamer called the *Silver Spray* ran aground on a limestone shoal here. It was on its way to pick up two hundred University of Chicago students and take them on a tour of Gary's steel mills.

After three days, the crew was rescued hours before waves broke the ship apart. Even a hot air balloon sailing overhead offered to help! Back on shore, rowdy onlookers built bonfires on the beach from the ship's wreckage.

The *Silver Spray* hit Morgan Shoal, a structure composed of 425-million-year-old limestone. About fourteen thousand years ago, glaciers carved sediment in the basin, leaving the limestone outcrop. The million-square-foot shelf of submerged rock is the remains of a coral reef that once extended to Niagara Falls, rivaling the Great Barrier

The *Silver Spray* had plenty of adventures on Lake Michigan before she came to rest there. In 1899, the ship's captain and engineer dismissed the rest of the crew and stole the steamer from a Michigan dock. The owner sent a tug boat to chase it down!

The seven-person crew refused to abandon the ship. According to the Chicago Examiner, *the cook was making Irish stew at the time and "not a man moved save the cook, who stirred some spice into the stew."*

SHIPWRECK OF THE *SILVER SPRAY*

WHAT A sign of life below

WHERE Lake Michigan at 49th Street Beach

COST Free

NOTEWORTHY Morgan Shoal's habitat is as close as Chicago gets to a wild coral reef.

Reef. In addition to the *Silver Spray*'s boiler, propeller, and drive shaft, the shoal is home to a unique aquatic ecosystem. Beneath the surface, the shoal's lush carpet of sea grass is thriving with aquatic life that you won't find elsewhere on the mostly sandy lake bed. It's even home to the longnose sucker, a threatened species in Illinois.

The shoal is a favorite with divers and snorkelers. Although the water drops to twenty feet off the shore, the area of the shoal is about five feet deep. The Chicago Park District once considered building land over the shoal, but thankfully it has preserved this exceptional ecosystem for Chicagoans. It's a world away, just a few feet from shore.

65 PROUD PERFORMANCE

Where can I attend an urban powwow?

Drums are pounding, colorful shawls twirl through the air, and every footstep is in sync. You're at a Native American powwow, not on a distant reservation, but in the middle of Chicago.

Powwows celebrate Indian traditions through the arts and share them with younger generations. A powwow consists of four circles. The drum is at the center surrounded by a ring of male singers, a ring of female singers, and a ring of everyone else at the event.

This rare, authentic Native American cultural experience is an American Indian Center tradition dating back to its founding in 1953. The center aims to promote fellowship between all tribes in Chicago and connection between Indians and non-Indians. Every year, the powwow welcomes the entire Chicago community to celebrate Native American culture through traditional dance, music, food, and artisans. More than 175 tribes from across the United States and Canada are represented.

In nearby Evanston, the Mitchell Museum of the American Indian highlights the history, culture, and arts of the North American native people. Its collection includes art and artifacts of American Indian and Inuit people from the Paleo-Indian period through the present day. American and Canadian cultures of the Woodlands, Plains, Southwest, Northwest Coast, and Arctic region are represented.

A Portage Park sculpture honors the Northwest Side's Native American heritage. Portage, by Ted Sitting Crow Garner, is a ten-foot-by-six-foot aluminum sculpture. A figure hoists a canoe on his back, referencing Portage Park's past as a swampy area between the Chicago and Des Plaines Rivers.

AMERICAN INDIAN CENTER

WHAT The country's oldest urban American Indian Center

WHERE 3401 W. Ainslie St.

COST Powwow admission is $10 for adults and $5 for seniors and kids six and up. Archery class is $20.

PRO TIP The Field Museum holds extensive collections of Hopewell, Plains, Northwest, and Southwest cultures.

In the 1950s, the Indian Relocation program moved thousands of American Indians from their reservations to Chicago. Chicago has the country's third-largest urban Native American population, and the community has centered around the Uptown neighborhood for decades. Today, Chicagoland's 65,000 American Indians are spread across six counties. The nation's oldest urban American Indian Center continues to be an important cultural resource for the community.

Another activity at the center that is popular with American Indians and non-Indians alike is archery. All-ages archery classes are available several nights per week.

Whatever your background, the American Indian Center offers many ways to celebrate Chicago's diversity. Come for the powwow and stay for the cultural heritage programs and Native American art. You might just become an expert archer along the way!

66

HIDDEN OASIS

Where can I find a restaurant gem hidden behind some actual gems?

Need some extra sparkle? Chicagoans have been coming to Wabash Avenue's historic Jewelers Row to get their gleam on since 1912. Unless you're in the habit of shopping for diamonds over lunch, however, you might not know it's also home to baba ghanouj.

Duck out of the elevated train racket overhead and into the Wabash Jewelers Mall. There's plenty to distract you in the mall's shimmering cases, but they keep the good stuff out back. Walk past the glittering diamonds, glowing pearls, and rows of watches to the rear of the building. That's where you'll smell chicken sizzling on the grill and spot the neon lights of the Oasis Café.

Even more surprising than a restaurant hidden behind a jewelry store is an affordable and delicious restaurant. The Oasis Café has been serving Middle Eastern specialties like

---

Home to jewelry manufacturers, wholesalers, and retailers, Jewelers Row was booming by World War II. In the 1980s, jewelry mogul Marshall Finkelman opened the Jewelers Mall to bring the world of international gem markets to Chicago. The market is home to jewelers from Mexico, South America, and Southeast Asia.

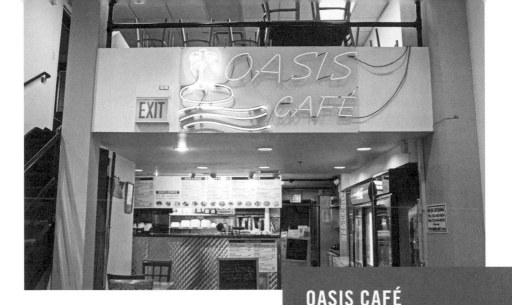

Believe it or not, you can find a bargain in the Jewelers Mall. The Oasis Café is hiding Middle Eastern eats at the rear of the building.

OASIS CAFÉ

WHAT A diamond in the rough

WHERE 21 N. Wabash Ave.

COST Items starting at $2.19

PRO TIP Signs on the front of the building direct hungry treasure hunters inside.

Moroccan chicken, kefta, and fattoush here for more than thirty years. Don't miss the daily specials like Moroccan couscous with sweet potatoes, zucchini, and spinach. If you're going for the gold, your best bet is the falafel sandwich. The classic, crispy dish is nestled in a fluffy pita and dressed in tahini. It's been ranked among the best in the Loop.

If you're looking for an unusual lunch in the Loop, head to the Oasis Café's open dining room and small balcony. The place can get packed around noon, so takeout is another option. All meals are under eleven dollars, so you'll have money left over to pick up a watch on the way out.

67

CAPTURE THE FLAG

Where do the Bulls and Blackhawks championship banners come from?

Sports fans know there's no feeling like watching your team's championship banner being raised after a hard-fought season. Yet most Bulls and Blackhawks fans don't realize that the banners at the United Center are made by the same family who has decorated Chicago for more than a century.

The banners' journey begins thirteen miles from the United Center, in the South Shore neighborhood. William George Newbould founded WGN Flag & Decorating Co. here in 1916, the same year President Woodrow Wilson established Flag Day. WGN Flag makes flags, signs, banners, bunting, pennants, and flagpoles found throughout Chicago and the suburbs.

The oldest family-owned flag company in the industry has been part of every major event in Chicago for more than one hundred years. In 1945, WGN draped the exterior of Marshall Field's in hundreds of flags and a giant bunting "V" for V-Day. When Queen Elizabeth visited Chicago in 1959, WGN decorated Navy Pier with five hundred yards of white

Chicagoans love their city flag, and you can find it decorating everything from t-shirts to tattoos. Each star and blue and white stripe has a meaning, but did you know that each star's six points have additional meanings?

In 2016, the city marked WGN Flag's one hundredth anniversary with the dedication of the honorary WGN Flag & Decorating Co. Avenue street sign.

WGN FLAG & DECORATING CO.

WHAT A century of decorating Chicago

WHERE 7984 S. Chicago Ave.

COST Free

NOTEWORTHY WGN Flag bears no relation to the WGN Chicago television or radio station.

satin. They have also helped the city mourn the deaths of Mayors Harold Washington and Richard J. Daley as well as Pope John Paul II and Cardinal Francis George.

According to fourth-generation owner Carl "Gus" Porter III, WGN Flag's proudest work hangs in the United Center. "As a fan of Chicago sports, our greatest pride comes from seeing these banners raised after a championship," he told *Voyage Chicago*. "People from all over the world are watching the ceremony, fixated on these banners that will be a permanent reminder of the sacrifice and fortitude of the teams."

WGN Flag's work appears on every block in Chicago. The next time you're walking down your street, take a moment to appreciate their century of Chicago craftsmanship.

68

GET ON YOUR SOAPBOX

Where can I hear Chicago's radicals speak?

Washington Square Park lies in the affluent Near North neighborhood adjacent to the esteemed Newberry Library. It's hard to believe this stately patch of green was once ground zero for oratory by Chicago's socialists, atheists, and eccentrics. One day a year, you can relive the park's radical past.

For decades, the park was known as Bughouse Square. "Bughouse" is slang for a mental health facility, and the freewheeling park often resembled a madhouse. Chicago's oldest public park got its start in the 1840s when a developer left his cow pasture to the city to become a park. A provision required a wall be built around it, so the city erected the short limestone barrier you see today. Another provision allowed anyone to make a speech in the park at any time.

People with something to say took advantage of this provision from the 1890s through the 1960s, filling the park nightly with passionate rants, theories, and debates and the hecklers who loved them. Bughouse regulars included preachers, anarchists, hobos, and screwballs. "One-Armed" Charlie Wendorf had the Constitution memorized and was considered the "mayor" of Bughouse Square. Sister Gracie would be overcome by religious ecstasies while on the

---

Another free speech forum, the College of Complexes, has been meeting weekly since 1951. "The Playground for People Who Think" is open to the public. Visit www.collegeofcomplexes.org for more info.

Bughouse Square was one of dozens of "free speech parks" in Chicago in the early twentieth century. Among the speakers who shouted from wooden crates in the square were Carl Sandburg, Clarence Darrow, Eugene Debs, and Studs Terkel. Every July, the Newberry Library revives the tradition at the Bughouse Square Debates.

BUGHOUSE SQUARE

WHAT Chicago's free speech forum

WHERE 901 N. Clark St.

COST Don't forget to tip when the hat is passed.

PRO TIP The Bughouse Square Debates are held during the Newberry Library Book Fair every July.

soapbox, while the "Cosmic Kid" took the audience on "flights of fancy into empyrean realms of thought."

By the 1960s, speeches in Bughouse Square had dwindled, possibly due to the rise of television. However, the right to speak in the park remains. Every July, the soapboxes return to the park for the annual Bughouse Square Debates. It's a public forum inviting people to encounter new ideas or mount the soapbox and share theirs. There's plenty of present-day material for Chicago's orators to convey, including healthcare policy, nuclear warfare, and UFOs.

In 1971, the *Chicago Tribune* interviewed a former Bughouse Square regular named Jimmie Sheridan. When asked whether he missed the old days at the square, Sheridan replied, "Don't need to. The whole world has become Bughouse Square."

69

ON THE RIGHT TRACK

Where can I have cocktails in a vintage train car?

Chicago is fortunate to have great public transportation, but a train that won't take you anywhere might be the best ticket in town. Many people step out of the Chicago Blue Line stop and wonder at the shiny silver train car permanently parked nearby. It's more than a prop. It's a bar car.

So how did a 132,000-pound train car end up in River West? Restaurateur David Gevercer purchased the train car in 2003. He installed a foundation and rails to hold the car, which was lowered onto the track by cranes. The eighty-five-by-ten-foot restaurant squeezed into a 120-by-twenty-five-foot lot. Crossing signals were installed near the sidewalk café.

The train has a history of serving hungry passengers. It was built as a dining car in 1947 for the Atlantic Coast Line Railroad. It ran on the railroad's twenty-five-hour-and-ten-minute run from New York to Miami on a train known as the Silver Palm. The car featured steak dinners on fine china and white linen, cocktails, and stainless steel ashtray stands.

After it landed in Chicago, the train car operated as a restaurant for several years. In 2008, Anthony Bourdain dined in the Silver Palm and declared its Three Little

---

Before pulling into Chicago, the train car endured a thirty-six-month journey from California via the Burlington Northern/Santa Fe and the Iowa Interstate Railroad.

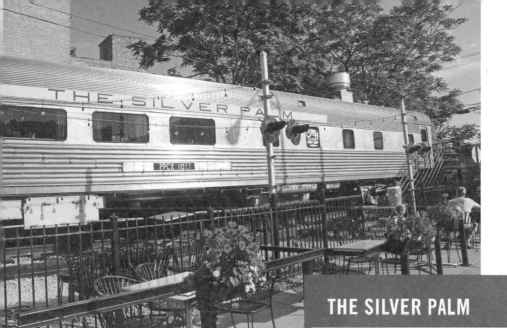

This stainless steel dining car was named The Washington when it served on the Atlantic Coast Line Railroad.

Pigs sandwich "the greatest sandwich in America." Today, the Silver Palm is a "bar car" remaining a one-of-a-kind location to enjoy a beer or classic cocktail.

The Silver Palm's sister establishment, the Matchbox, is also a Chicago notable. Known as Chicago's "most intimate bar," the Matchbox is the city's smallest bar at 460 square feet. It boasts a lively atmosphere and a seventy-five-year-old cocktail pedigree. Only about twenty people can fit into the triangle-shaped space, but outdoor patios accommodate many more.

If you're looking to be transported to a unique drinking experience complete with vintage nostalgia and classic cocktails, then all aboard The Silver Palm!

70

SMILE LIKE YOU MEAN IT

Why are the water towers in Calumet City so happy?

It's easy to look on the bright side of life when you have 140-foot-tall reminders. The citizens of Calumet City have been smiling since 1973 when a youngster suggested painting smiley faces on the town's water towers.

Smiley faces were ubiquitous in the early 1970s, plastering everything from dishes to buttons. Where other people saw mundane water towers, eight-year-old Kim Fornero saw a blank canvas. She wrote to former mayor Robert Stefaniak saying she could see the water tower from her house and that it would look cute with a smiley face on it. The city council agreed and painted the daily reminder to smile as a kind of community billboard.

SMILING WATER TOWERS

WHAT A pair of larger-than-life emojis

WHERE 96 River Oaks Center Dr. and Paxton Ave. at 142nd St., Calumet City, IL

COST Free

NOTEWORTHY John Belushi and Dan Aykroyd's characters in *The Blues Brothers* were born in Calumet City and grew up in the orphanage there.

The smiling water tower at River Oaks Shopping Center has a bowtie painted on its neck to signify its identity as "Mr. Smiley Face." Another happy water tower without a tie, known as "Mrs. Smiley Face," followed on the Calumet Expressway.

The towers have become a symbol of Calumet City, attracting outside attention over the years. The grinning faces are featured in the 1990 Black Crowes music video for

Calumet City claims to be the first town to paint a smiley face on its water tower. The town "got happy" in 1973.

"Hard to Handle" as well as a Nine Inch Nails music video and a scene in the film *Natural Born Killers*. A photo of the water tower also appears on the back of the Dead Kennedys album *Plastic Surgery Disasters*.

The groovy grin of the smiley water towers might seem outdated to some, but looking on the bright side will never go out of style.

Other Illinois cities soon debuted artistic water towers, including the giant rose tower in Rosemont, Orland Park's teed golf ball tower, and a leafy branch in Forest Park. Atlanta, Makanda, and Watseka, Illinois, continued the smiley face theme.

71

SECRET CIVIL WAR

Is Chicago home to the largest mass grave in the Western Hemisphere?

There were no Civil War battles fought in Illinois, but the Land of Lincoln is home to significant reminders of the era. A plaque at Lake Street and Wacker Drive marks the site of the "Wigwam," where Lincoln won the Republican presidential nomination. History buffs can see the table where Robert E. Lee signed the war surrender terms as well as Lincoln's deathbed at the Chicago History Museum. Yet one deadly chapter of Chicago's role in the war is commonly overlooked.

Most Chicagoans don't know that Bronzeville was the site of a Confederate prison camp during the Civil War. Camp Douglas was named for Illinois senator Stephen Douglas, who donated his land for the camp at 31st Street between Cottage Grove Avenue and today's Martin Luther King Jr. Drive. It opened in 1861 as a Union army training camp but soon started housing captured Confederate soldiers.

As the war raged on, the camp built for six thousand prisoners swelled to twelve thousand. Living conditions plummeted as overcrowding, swampy ground, and poor sanitation spread disease among the inmates. More deaths occurred at Camp Douglas than at any of the other 150 Union prison camps. Camp Douglas was nicknamed "eighty

---

Oak Woods Cemetery is the final resting place for several notable Chicagoans, including Thomas A. Dorsey, Enrico Fermi, Jesse Owens, and Chicago's first African American mayor, Harold Washington.

Camp Douglas claimed more Confederate lives than any other Union prison camp. The monument marking their mass grave is located in Section K near the cemetery's southwest corner.

OAK WOODS CEMETERY

WHAT The Western Hemisphere's largest mass grave

WHERE 1035 E. 67th St.

COST Free

NOTEWORTHY Among the soldiers who enlisted in the Union army at Camp Douglas were African Americans who fought with Companies B and C of the 29th US Colored Infantry.

acres of hell." By the time the camp closed in 1865, more than forty thousand troops had passed through it.

More than four thousand Confederate soldiers who died at Camp Douglas were eventually buried in a mass grave at Oak Woods Cemetery. A towering thirty-foot monument inscribed with each soldier's name marks the site. The solemn plot also includes four cannons, a pyramid of cannonballs, and twelve headstones marking the graves of unknown Union camp guards. Nearby, a cenotaph memorializes Southerners who stood with the Union. As Camp Douglas Restoration Foundation founder David Keller told the *Tribune* in 2015, "It is part of our heritage—a dark part but nevertheless important in many different ways."

72

WAIT A MINUTE, MR. POSTMAN

Are historic artworks hidden inside Chicago post offices?

Few people look forward to visiting the post office. Yet residents in several Chicago neighborhoods disagree. Rather than long lines and grumpy staff, they encounter historic artworks by some of the most talented artists of the last century.

The Lakeview Post Office is one such building. Visitors are immediately struck by a twenty-four-foot-long mural above the counter. Harry Sternberg created *Epic (Epoch) of a Great City* in 1937. It depicts the perseverance of Chicago from its Fort Dearborn days, through the Great Chicago Fire, and into the industrial era that gave rise to its monumental growth. Laborers in a mill, factory, farm, and the stockyards strike a heroic pose as they propel the city forward.

This stunning surprise isn't the only such mural in Chicago's post offices. During the Great Depression, the Federal Art Project (FAP) provided some five thousand jobs by funding public art projects. Artists were selected through competitions and commissioned to create

The Chicago Public Schools are home to the largest remaining collection of Works Progress Administration (WPA) and pre-Depression murals in America. More than four hundred murals, dating from 1904 to 1943, still exist in the Chicago Public Schools.

Sternberg's mural was restored in 2003, thanks to members of the community. Friends of the Lakeview Post Office raised sixteen thousand dollars to revive this piece of Chicago history. The restoration work took place during business hours so neighbors could watch the hidden treasure come to life.

LAKEVIEW POST OFFICE

WHAT Art worth writing home about

WHERE 1343 W. Irving Park Rd.

COST Free

PRO TIP Sternberg painted himself into the Lakeview mural. Look for the worker wearing a leather apron.

works celebrating American life. Sadly, many of these Depression-era pieces were lost to time and neglect.

Lakeview isn't the only neighborhood whose post office harbors artistic treasures. In Uptown, a ceramic tile mural by Henry Varnum Poor celebrates the people and history of Chicago. One panel portrays iconic Chicago poet Carl Sandburg, who lived in nearby Ravenswood. Another panel depicts architect Louis Sullivan planning his Carson Pirie Scott Building amidst a growing Chicago. In Logan Square, the post office features a 1937 Art Deco sculpture called *The Post*.

By placing this art in post offices, it became accessible to people of all walks of life. Other Chicago post offices that feature FAP art include the Central Annex, Kedzie-Grace, Loop, and Morgan Park. If you can't make it to a museum, admire these historic records of American history the next time you ship something.

73

TOO CLOSE FOR COMFORT

Does the Goodman Theatre own the skull of a comedy legend?

The Goodman Theatre has seen many dramatic acts. Yet one of its most infamous scenes took place offstage in 1999, when the theatre was presented with a human skull to use in future productions of *Hamlet*. The origin of the skull was a secret that took seven years to uncover.

In 1997, Second City veteran and ImprovOlympic founder Del Close added a clause to his will bequeathing his skull to the Goodman Theatre. The comedy legend wanted to continue his career beyond the veil by leaving his skull to play Yorick in *Hamlet,* or "for any purposes it deems appropriate."

Before he died from emphysema, Close repeated his wishes to his professional partner Charna Halpern. According to her 2006 *New Yorker* interview, he said, "Promise me you'll make the skull thing happen no matter what." A few months later, the skull was sitting on a red velvet cushion in a Lucite case and entrusted to the Goodman in a public ceremony. Artistic director Robert Falls held up the skull and said, "Alas, poor Yorick, I knew you Del."

There were rumors, however, that the skull didn't belong to Close. For starters, it was held together with rusty screws. It also had teeth, even though Close wore dentures.

GOODMAN THEATRE

WHAT A funny bone

WHERE 170 N. Dearborn St.

COST Theater tickets run from $10 to $75.

PRO TIP The skull is stored in a private office.

The last day of Close's life in 1999 was a show like none other. He celebrated his birthday at Illinois Masonic Hospital among friends and former students. He invited pagan priests to chant him into the next life. Bill Murray hired a saxophone player for the occasion. The Upright Citizens Brigade sent a Comedy Central camera crew to film the festivities.

In 2006, Halpern finally admitted that the skull wasn't Close's. The hospital had refused her request to cut off his head so Halpern did some improvising of her own. She visited a medical supply company and chose a "manly, manly skull" to stand in for Close's. She and her sister even pulled some of the skull's teeth to make it more closely resemble Close.

While the skull might not technically have belonged to the master of improv, it's a symbol of his eccentric legacy. As usual, Del Close had the last laugh.

In his forty-plus-year comedy career, Del Close's students included the likes of Harold Ramis, Gilda Radner, John Belushi, Dan Aykroyd, Mike Myers, Chris Farley, Stephen Colbert, and Amy Poehler.

74

FIT TO BE TIED

Where can I find a collection of antique sexual accessories?

The Midwest may be known as conservative, but Chicago was home to the nation's first leather bar. The Gold Coast bar opened in 1958, catering to the leather community. Today, the Leather Archives and Museum celebrates that history and subculture in an institution that contains some of Chicago's raciest artifacts.

"Leather" refers to those who participate in unconventional expressions of eroticism and sexual behavior. The ten-thousand-square-foot Rogers Park museum features several exhibition galleries, a research library, an auditorium, and archives.

The titillating museum tours the history of leather culture, including BDSM, kink, fetish, LGBTQ, and straight interests. Those looking for vintage sex equipment will get an eyeful of crops, handcuffs, whips, and chastity devices. In addition to the museum's namesake leather objects on display, a jaw-dropping collection of art, video, and writing brings the movement to life. Visitors can view the artwork of the world-famous Tom of Finland as well as the world's largest collection of work by Chicago painter Etienne. The collection of club uniforms, banners, and patches traces the

Just a few blocks away, the Gerber/Hart Library and Archives is the Midwest's largest LGBTQ circulating library. Founded in 1981, the library has amassed more than fourteen thousand volumes.

The museum features a dungeon complete with an authentic dominatrix costume, a spanking apparatus, and antique sexual devices.

LEATHER ARCHIVES AND MUSEUM

WHAT The world's first archival collection of the leather subculture

COST $10 admission, $5 for students, free for members

PRO TIP The museum exhibitions and library are open to the public (eighteen years of age and older).

community's reach. Exhibits range from transgender leather history to bootblacking to bondage safety.

"Our primary purpose is to give grounding and history to people who are already in the [leather] community," former executive director Joseph Bean told the *Tribune* in 2000. "It's a pride thing, a heritage thing."

Chicago is also home to International Mr. Leather, the world's largest leather contest and conference. Mr. Leather's duties include educating queer and straight enthusiasts about BDSM culture.

The BDSM community is a secret no more, thanks to this preservation of its history and diversity. Visit the Leather Archives and Museum to get educated or inspired—just keep the community mantra in mind: "safe, sane, and consensual."

75 TINY TOWN

Where is Chicago's smallest neighborhood?

Chicago is divided into seventy-seven official community areas, containing neighborhoods and pocket neighborhoods with sometimes shifting names and borders. Tucked into Irving Park on the Northwest Side is a hidden, historic neighborhood called the Villa District.

This micro neighborhood consists of only 126 single-family homes on a triangle-shaped plot between Avondale, Addison, Pulaski, and Hamlin Streets. Irving Park was named after author Washington Irving, and the Villa District was originally called "Irving Park Villa." The Villa was built for wealthy Chicagoans as an escape from the congestion of the city. Residents could enjoy its bucolic boulevards while maintaining access to the city via the nearby train and streetcar lines.

The Villa was one of Chicago's first planned developments. Unlike today's cookie-cutter suburbs, it was designed with character in mind. The original owner of the land included covenants forbidding flat roofs, apartment buildings, commercial establishments, and two houses looking the same. Marketing materials for the Villa promised "light, air, and beauty," and the neighborhood delivered with fifty-foot-wide lots, twice the Chicago standard.

Chicagoans can thank the Villa Improvement League for preserving the architecture of this tiny community since 1907. It's the city's oldest continuously operating neighborhood association.

Left, *The original marketing materials described the Villa District as "the Park in Irving Park," "the beauty spot of the Northwest Side," and "a home in a park."* Right, *The Villa District is known for its stone pillars at every street corner. The five-foot-tall pillars were originally built as light stands topped with globe fixtures. They were transformed into planters in 1923 and are maintained by volunteers from the Villa Improvement League.*

The Villa owes its distinctive feel to its delightful hodgepodge of Prairie-style, Tudor, and Craftsman bungalows built between 1907 and 1922. Stone pillars mark every corner in the Villa, and landscaped medians run the length of some streets. The area earned a spot on the National Register of Historic Places and is a City of Chicago Historic Landmark District.

Journalist Mike Royko nicknamed the Villa District "Polish Kenilworth" after the swanky suburb. The neighborhood was built as a retreat, and as you walk the leafy streets today it's easy to forget that you're next to an expressway. For a while, you can still retreat into the early twentieth century.

76

FIELD OF DREAMS

What Chicago ballpark trained both Madonna and Michael Jordan?

The Illinois Institute of Technology is better known for science and engineering than athletics, but it does boast several Division III teams. The Scarlet Hawks' baseball diamond is located just a half mile from the White Sox's ballpark, closer than that of any other university to a major league field. While you might not recognize any team veterans, the field has hosted some famous names that will surprise you.

Remember when Michael Jordan retired from basketball and played baseball? To prepare for the league, Jordan came to train at IIT with veteran coach Jim Darrah. Darrah coached Jordan in the finer points of outfielding and praised his determination. "He goofed me up in a drill I use for my guys where they can't get to balls," Darrah told the *Chicago Sun-Times* in 1994. "I think I got it far enough away from him and he glides after it. He said, 'You have to throw them to the parking lot for me not to get it.'" The result? Jordan signed with the White Sox and played a season in the minor leagues.

The All-American Girls League, depicted in the film *A League of Their Own*, was formed in 1943, followed by the National Girls Baseball League in 1944. While most of their stadiums did not survive after both leagues closed in 1954, Thillens Stadium still stands at Devon and Kedzie.

While it's home to IIT's baseball team, many famous names have taken the field over the years. In 1993, White Sox players Bo Jackson and Ozzie Guillen trained here to rehabilitate from injuries. Bo Jackson threw out the first pitch of the Scarlet Hawks' spring 1996 season.

ED GLANCY FIELD AT ILLINOIS INSTITUTE OF TECHNOLOGY

WHAT Baseball training ground to the stars

WHERE 3300 S. Federal St.

COST Free

PRO TIP The Scarlet Hawks typically play a home game once a season at the White Sox field.

Coach Darrah has trained some other big names with baseball aspirations. In 1992, Madonna, Geena Davis, and Tom Hanks frequented the IIT field to prepare for their film *A League of Their Own*. Madonna may not have been a baseball natural, but per Darrah, she stepped up to the plate. "What she lacked in baseball skills she made up for in determination. She stayed after everybody left and really worked at it."

In a city of legendary stadiums and baseball lore, IIT flies under the radar. Check out the Scarlet Hawks' schedule this season to enjoy some quality baseball without the crowds and ticket prices of Chicago's bigger ballparks.

77

WALK THE LINE

Is Chicago's historic boundary hidden in plain sight?

Rogers Park is Chicago's most diverse neighborhood, home to residents who speak nearly forty languages and hail from more than eighty countries. Yet long before the rest of us arrived, the region was home to Native Americans. A historic border from Chicago's days as a frontier town remains in Rogers Park, if you know where to look.

The diagonal Rogers Avenue is a bit of living history. It originated as an ancient Native American trail, and it marked the northern boundary between native and white settler lands. The Treaty of St. Louis established this trail as the Indian Boundary Line in 1816, allowing settlers south and east of the line. The Council of Three Fires, including the Ojibwa, Ottawa, and Pottawatomie tribes, ceded a twenty-mile-by-seventy-mile corridor of land. Among those signing the treaty on behalf of the United States were the first governor of Illinois and William Clark of the Lewis and Clark Expedition. Clark's brother, George Rogers Clark, was a Revolutionary War hero after whom Clark Street was named.

This treaty didn't last long. In 1833, the Treaty of Chicago drove Native Americans out of the area. You can still trace the treaty line of Rogers Avenue from Eastlake Terrace

---

The Treaty of St. Louis gave the United States a tract of land from Lake Michigan to the Illinois River, including the property to build the Illinois and Michigan Canal.

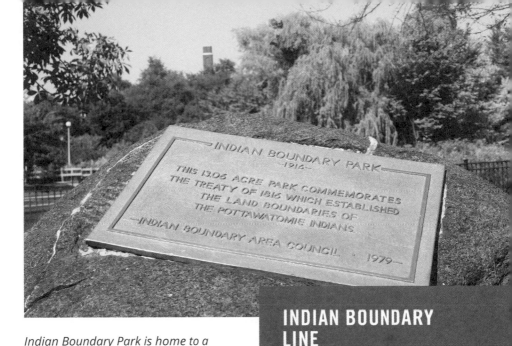

THIS 13.06 ACRE PARK COMMEMORATES
THE TREATY OF 1816 WHICH ESTABLISHED
THE LAND BOUNDARIES OF
THE POTTAWATOMIE INDIANS

—INDIAN BOUNDARY PARK—
-1916-

—INDIAN BOUNDARY AREA COUNCIL · 1979—

Indian Boundary Park is home to a fieldhouse featuring decorative Native American reliefs throughout. A pair of boulders in the park display plaques telling the story of the play lot and the Indian Boundary Line.

INDIAN BOUNDARY LINE

WHAT A hidden historic marker

WHERE N. Clark St. and N. Rogers Ave.

COST Free

NOTEWORTHY Rogers Avenue is named in honor of the same man after whom the community of Rogers Park is named, Philip Rogers.

to Ridge Boulevard, starting and stopping a bit before it becomes Forest Preserve Drive.

A plaque installed at Clark Street and Rogers Avenue in 1937 commemorates the historic boundary, but you won't see it at first glance. The city honored this bit of history by installing a green traffic light controller directly in front of the plaque! If you head to the intersection's northeast corner, you can still read it.

Indian Boundary Park in nearby West Ridge also commemorates the dividing line. The 13.6-acre park lies in the path of the trail. We can't change history, but at least we can walk in its footsteps.

78

ON THE MOVE

Does a statue at Graceland Cemetery disappear at night?

As final resting places go, Graceland Cemetery is among the best. The 119-acre park stretches across North Side neighborhoods in a swath of landscaped lanes and lagoons. It's no wonder some of Chicago's most notable names, including Potter Palmer, Marshall Field, and George Pullman, are buried there. Yet one of Graceland's most famous residents wasn't a titan of industry but a six-year-old girl, and some say that she also explores the cemetery.

The grave of Inez Clarke is easy to spot near the center of the cemetery. It's marked by the statue of a smiling girl seated and holding a parasol that rests on a stone pedestal. The entire statue is enclosed in a glass case, keeping it remarkably well preserved. A plaque reads "Inez Clarke 1873–1880."

Although Inez has been buried here for more than 130 years, it seems she has a restless spirit. Security guards have reported the statue vanishing during the night and reappearing the next morning. According to legend, the statue regularly comes to life to wander the cemetery.

Yet that's not Inez's only secret. Some historians claim she isn't buried there at all. A mix-up in cemetery records

Graceland is the final resting place for Chicago's most noted architects. Residents include Daniel Burnham, Louis Sullivan, Howard Van Doren Shaw, Ludwig Mies van der Rohe, and photographer Richard Nickel.

Left, *According to legend, Inez Clarke was struck by lightning and killed at the age of six. She is said to haunt Graceland Cemetery, especially during storms. The death certificate for Inez Briggs says that she died of diphtheria.* Right, *One of Graceland Cemetery's most recognizable residents is Lorado Taft's brooding 1909 sculpture,* Eternal Silence. *It was commissioned by the descendants of Chicago pioneer Dexter Graves. Nicknamed the Statue of Death, it's said that if a person looks into the sculpture's eyes, they will see a vision of their own death.*

GRACELAND CEMETERY

WHAT A monument on the move

WHERE 4001 N. Clark St.

COST Free

PRO TIP Graceland's park-like setting is a beautiful place to stroll, if you don't mind the departed company.

has led researchers to believe the grave may belong to a girl named Inez Briggs or even a young boy named Amos Briggs. Another theory claims that the statue isn't a tribute to a departed child, but an advertisement. The sculptor A. Gagel, whose name appears on the statue, may have placed the monument here to promote his business.

Whether Inez Clarke is buried here and why she might be compelled to wander the grounds are secrets she's taken to the grave.

79 CLOSE ENCOUNTERS OF THE CHICAGO KIND

Are the world's greatest UFO secrets stored in Chicago?

Chicago is home to many unexplained mysteries, but perhaps none are as puzzling as those housed by the J. Allen Hynek Center for UFO Studies. How did the first national organization dedicated to the scientific study of UFOs land in Chicago instead of, say, Washington, D.C., or even Roswell?

The center's namesake, Dr. Hynek, established the Center for UFO Studies (CUFOS) in 1973. It serves to maintain a library and archives of UFO-related materials, including reports, books, articles, and a database of UFO sightings. The center supports ongoing investigations by providing research materials, while continuing to conduct its own evaluations of UFO sightings around the world.

Dr. Hynek was an esteemed astronomer and professor who helped the US government develop defense technology during World War II and worked to establish the nation's satellite program. Hynek started out as a UFO skeptic. He was hired as an astronomical consultant by the US Air Force to participate in three separate UFO debunking investigations between the 1940s and the 1960s. The investigations were called Project Sign, Project Grudge, and Project Blue Book.

Although he could provide an astronomical explanation for 80 percent of sightings,

J. ALLEN HYNEK CENTER FOR UFO STUDIES

WHAT A private research center

WHERE Online or by appointment

COST Free

PRO TIP Much of CUFOS's work is available at cufos.org. Serious researchers may visit the archives by appointment.

In 1972, Hynek coined the phrase "close encounters" in his book The UFO Experience: A Scientific Inquiry, *in which he describes categories for classifying UFO sightings.*

such as mistaken planets or meteors, there was a small percentage of unexplained cases. As postwar UFO mania increased, the government sought to silence the sightings. Over time, Dr. Hynek believed that UFOs deserved serious scientific investigation. He wrote three books on the subject and even coined the term "close encounter" to describe extraterrestrial meetings.

Hynek was a professor at Northwestern University when he founded CUFOS to encourage the scientific community to work together studying UFO cases by employing scientific analysis. The next time someone tells you they've seen something they can't explain, keep Dr. Hynek's words in mind: "Ridicule is not part of the scientific method, and people should not be taught that it is."

Steven Spielberg borrowed more than Hynek's terminology for his 1977 film Close Encounters of the Third Kind. Dr. Hynek was a consultant on the film, and he can be seen in the closing scene of the film as the bearded man with a pipe.

80

THE LAST PIONEER

Did this old man make a thirty-year stand against the City of Chicago?

Among Streeterville's tangle of tall glass buildings, you'll find a dapper old man. He's jauntily dressed in a top hat and holds a small dog, but the playful grin behind his mustache suggests he's anything but harmless. Does this look like someone who defied the city's police and tycoons for thirty years?

The eight-foot bronze sculpture honors Captain George "Cap" Wellington Streeter, described on the plaque as "the eccentric resident who gave Streeterville its name." It doesn't mention that he did so in a most Chicago fashion.

In 1886, Streeter's steamship hit a storm in Lake Michigan and washed up on a sandbar around Superior Street. The sandbar grew around the boat as Streeter invited locals to dump trash on the site, creating 186 acres of lakeshore land in the process. He sold plots of this new land, forming a shantytown. Streeter named the ramshackle area between the mouth of the Chicago River and Oak Street the "District of Lake Michigan." He claimed the "Deestrict" as his own, declaring it was not subject to Chicago or Illinois laws since it was west of the documented shoreline.

According to legend, Streeter's last words were a curse on the city of Chicago and its politicians for their actions against him. Some believe the Streeterville curse is responsible for unexplained happenings in the John Hancock Center.

"Cap" Streeter founded Streeterville on landfill. In 1900, Streeter raised a ragtag army after a group of men burned his house down. More than four hundred police and sixteen patrol wagons surrounded the district in a standoff.

"CAP" STREETER SCULPTURE

WHAT A Chicago original

WHERE Corner of McClurg Ct. and Grand Ave.

COST Free

NOTEWORTHY The sculpture is the work of Illinois artist Dennis Downes.

The wealthy lakefront neighbors, including Potter Palmer, were not pleased with Streeter's squatting and selling liquor on Sundays. The accounts of their decades-long dispute read like slapstick. Officials serving him eviction papers were shot in their behinds with pellets, and police were drenched in boiling water. Streeter once held a police station hostage until they agreed to return guns they had stolen from his home. Somehow, Streeter was always acquitted of any charges.

Finally, the courts ruled in 1918 that he had no claim to the land now known as Streeterville. When the city's "last pioneer" was buried in 1921, even the mayor attended his funeral. As the *Tribune* said, "He was an original, amusing, and picturesque figure in the life of Chicago."

81

FIT FOR A KING

What's a pyramid doing in Chicagoland?

All that glitters isn't gold, but it does stop traffic. Drivers on I-94 may do a double take passing through Wadsworth, Illinois. You're not in the desert, and that's not a mirage. It's a giant pyramid surrounded by a moat.

The pharaoh who calls this place home is Jim Onan. He and his wife, Linda, built the complex in 1977 and raised their family here. According to their website, the Onans were inspired by "power, gold, and mystery." In the 1970s, theories circulated about magical powers related to pyramids generating their own energy, and the Onans wanted to channel that energy.

Visiting the bizarre home is unexpectedly educational. A fifty-five-foot statue of Ramses II greets visitors. You'll cross the moat leading to the six-story, seventeen-thousand-square-foot pyramid. Inside, the Onans display Egyptian murals and authentic artifacts like a Third Dynasty cuneiform tablet and an Eighteenth Dynasty oil lamp in a mini-museum. The theme continues in the family's living quarters. One room contains gold chairs that once belonged to *Ten Commandments* producer Cecil B. DeMille.

"I've been around pyramids my entire life," says Rocko Onan, Jim and Linda's son. "It's only when I go to other people's houses that it seems weird."

A small Egyptian-inspired gift shop offers treasures for the modern Indiana Jones. Most curiously, it sells Gold Pyramid Water, made from water that flows in a natural spring under the house. It doesn't claim to have any healing effects.

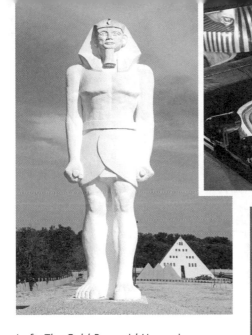

Left, *The Gold Pyramid House is a one-ninth scale reproduction of the Great Pyramid of Giza. At one time, it was the largest gold-plated object in the world.* Right, *The property also boasts an exact replica of King Tutankhamun's tomb.*

GOLD PYRAMID HOUSE

WHAT Once the world's largest gold structure

WHERE 37921 N. Dilleys Rd., Wadsworth, IL

COST The grounds are free to visit. Admission to evening concerts is $10.

NOTEWORTHY Rather than a three-car garage, the Onans have a three-pyramid garage.

If you think the pyramid is impressive, you should have seen it when it was really shining. The house was once covered in four thousand plates made of twenty-four-karat gold and was listed in the *Guinness Book of World Records* as the world's largest gold structure. The gold plating was removed after neighbors complained it was blinding. These days, the pyramid's sunny exterior comes from gold-colored paint.

The house is under renovation after suffering a fire in 2018 and tours are on hold. However, the Onans continue to host outdoor concerts and events on their property. The pyramid is living proof of the family's passion for ancient Egypt. It's certainly one of the most distinctive homes this side of Giza.

82

PIPE DREAMS

Is there a tobacco sanctuary in Chicago's Loop?

The days of TV dads, philosophers, and even Mr. Potato Head puffing on pipes may be history, but there's one place in the Loop where you can still smoke in style. Iwan Ries & Co. has been selling tobacco since before the Civil War, making it America's oldest family-owned tobacco shop. They also operate the Loop's only smoking lounge.

The business was founded in 1857, just a few decades after the city itself. German immigrant Edward Hoffman established the eponymous shop and recruited his nephew Iwan Ries to help him run the growing business. Iwan later took over and changed the shop's name with his uncle's blessing. The business has stayed in the family and is currently run by its fourth and fifth generations.

The scent of cigar smoke is infused in the lobby's wood-paneled walls. Visitors to Iwan Ries have their choice of more than one hundred brands and one thousand varieties of tobacco. Glass cases display more than fifteen thousand handsome pipes neatly lining the walls. The pipes range from fifteen-dollar corncobs to a $1,200 pipe handcrafted by German maestro Rainer Barbi. The shop also houses a collection of antique pipes and smoking paraphernalia, including an eighteenth-century Turkish water pipe and a

Iwan Ries has a connection to virtually all pipe and cigar smokers in Chicago history. For example, they delivered tobacco to officers residing at Camp Douglas during the Civil War.

During the golden age of pipe smoking in the 1950s, Iwan Ries & Co. and its Three Star Blue tobacco brand were household names. The business was also the first to offer a catalog and mail-order service to pipe smokers around the world.

IWAN RIES & CO.

WHAT The Loop's only smoking lounge

WHERE 19 S. Wabash Ave.

COST A smoking lounge membership is $750 annually or $15 for a single day.

PRO TIP Don't miss the store's 175-year-old wooden cigar store Indian.

blackened piece that survived the original store's destruction in the Great Chicago Fire.

Iwan Ries's longevity grandfathered in their ability to operate a smoking lounge despite the 2008 smoking ban in Chicago's public places. The introspective smoking set takes refuge in the elegant lounge's three rooms located in architect Louis Sullivan's oldest surviving building. Lounge members puff away in leather chairs among carved woodwork and sparkling chandeliers. The windows frame the "L" train rambling past while members play chess and sip on BYOB refreshments. Some members have private humidor lockers. After 160 years of serving tobacco enthusiasts, Iwan Ries and its smoking lounge are a modern take on Chicago's lost cigar bars.

83 EYE CAN SEE CLEARLY NOW

Where can you get prescription glasses for a giant?

There's always one neighbor who's been around since before anyone can remember. In West Lawn, he stands head and shoulders above the rest.

An enormous tobacco store Indian sculpture keeps watch on the intersection of 63rd Street and Pulaski Avenue from his perch on top of the Midwest Eye Clinic. Locally known as "the Chief," he raises one arm in a greeting while the other is at his side. The feather he used to wear on top of his head was damaged long ago, but he does sport a sign on his chest reading "Eye Can See Now."

The fourteen-foot-tall sculpture arrived on the Southwest Side in 1966. During that heyday of car travel, giant fiberglass figures popped up along roadsides across the country to lure passing motorists with their advertisements.

The Indian originally stood atop the Capitol Cigar Store advertising its White Owl Cigars. After several decades promoting tobacco, the vision center opened in the space. In recent years, they even fashioned a giant pair of glasses for their mascot. He must need quite a prescription!

EYE CARE INDIAN

WHAT A bespeckled brave

WHERE 6254 S. Pulaski Rd.

COST Free

NOTEWORTHY The sculpture was featured in the opening driving scene of the 1992 film *Wayne's World*.

Is the Chief extending a greeting or halting traffic on 63rd Street? Either way, you can't miss him.

It turns out the Indian has a cheeky side, specifically the southwest side of the intersection. If you view him from this side of 63rd Street, you'll notice that his resting hand appears to resemble another part of the anatomy. While this Midcentury advertising strategy isn't culturally sensitive, the neighborhood landmark continues to stop traffic.

Want a photo of the big guy? Stop by Marquette Photo Supply a few blocks east at 3314 West 63rd Street. Joe and Barbara Herbert have been running the shop since 1945.

84

ALL THAT JAZZ

Can I sit in Al Capone's booth at the Green Mill?

The glittering neon sign at the corner of Lawrence and Broadway welcomes visitors to the Green Mill, Chicago's most storied bar. Since 1907, it has hosted movie stars, gangsters, and jazz greats. If you want to explore the history of this legendary space, there's one seat in the house you can't miss.

The Green Mill began as Pop Morse's Roadhouse. It was renamed the Green Mill Gardens in 1910. A small windmill on the roof referenced Paris's Moulin Rouge. It's now the oldest nightclub in Chicago operating under the same name.

Today's Green Mill was part of an entertainment complex including ballrooms and gardens. People tied their horses to a hitching post outside. Some of those saddling up to the bar were silent film stars from nearby Essanay Studios, like Charlie Chaplin, Gloria Swanson, and "Bronco Billy" Anderson.

During Prohibition, the Green Mill became a hangout for gangsters. "Machine Gun" Jack McGurn was a part owner, and Al Capone was often found in the corner booth at the end of the bar. From this spot, he could see both doors and

---

A place this legendary can make anyone poetic. In 1986, poet Marc Smith invented the poetry slam at the Green Mill. Since then, the competitive poetry performances have spread around the world. The Uptown Poetry Slam still takes place at the Green Mill every Sunday night.

The Green Mill's stage is the stuff of legend. Everyone including Al Jolson, Billie Holiday, Benny Goodman, Ella Fitzgerald, and Kurt Elling has performed there.

GREEN MILL

WHAT Where the Jazz Age reigns

WHERE 4802 N. Broadway St.

COST The cover ranges from $5 to $15.

PRO TIP Shhh! If you talk during performances, the crowd and staff will let you hear it.

the stage. Whenever Capone walked in, the band stopped what they were doing to play "Rhapsody in Blue." When the gang needed a quick exit, they opened a trapdoor behind the bar and escaped through the basement into underground tunnels.

When the Green Mill's brightest star, singer Joe E. Lewis, took a job elsewhere, McGurn reacted by slitting the performer's throat and cutting off part of his tongue. Lewis survived and returned to the Green Mill stage years later as a comic. A framed poem behind the bar illustrates this incident.

This jazz joint still jumps with live music every night of the week. Grab a drink at the curving wooden bar, settle into a green velvet booth, and brush up on your local history before the band starts.

85

GRAVE MISTAKE

How do you lose 38,000 graves?

"Be careful, or you're going to Dunning." Chicago parents used this threat for decades to stop naughty children in their tracks. The thought of going to the poorhouse and insane asylum was enough to scare any delinquent straight. Thousands of Chicago's most unfortunate citizens went to Dunning . . . and many never left.

Starting in 1854, the Dunning complex operated on 320 acres in present-day Portage Park. What started as a poor farm grew to include a tuberculosis hospital and the Cook County Insane Asylum. It also included graves—lots of them. Cemeteries were built on the property to bury Dunning residents, Civil War veterans, unclaimed victims of the Great Chicago Fire, and bodies moved from the Lincoln Park potter's field after the closing of City Cemetery.

Life at Dunning was about as miserable as you'd expect a nineteenth-century insane asylum to be. Eventually, the asylum and poorhouse moved. The facilities were torn down, and the tragic stories of an estimated 38,000 people buried at Dunning were forgotten. Their mostly unmarked graves, including infants, orphans, and unknown adults, were erased from the landscape.

The hospital complex was nicknamed after the nearby Dunning Station. Built in 1882, the Chicago, Milwaukee & St. Paul Railway extended a line to transport supplies, medicine, and patients. According to legend, this is where the term "crazy train" originated.

UNKNOWN AND ITINERANT
POOR OF COOK COUNTY

UNIDENTIFIED VICTIMS OF TRAGEDY AND ALL
OTHERS NOT CLAIMED FOR BURIAL FROM THE
CHICAGO CITY MORGUE, ARE INTERRED IN
THIS CEMETERY AT DUNNING. WHILE
ABANDONED IN LIFE, EACH, IN DEATH, WAS
ALLOWED A FINAL RESTING PLACE IN THIS
CEMETERY.

In 2016, planned work on Oak Park Avenue was halted when about one thousand bodies were discovered buried under the road. The road was moved east to avoid disturbing the corpses. Although they were the city's most overlooked people in life, Dunning's departed now have the power to impact modern Chicago.

READ DUNNING MEMORIAL PARK

WHAT A forgotten graveyard

WHERE 6596 W. Belle Plaine Ave.

COST Free

NOTEWORTHY Amazingly, Chicago has more than one park built on a graveyard. Lincoln Park is built on the grounds of the former Chicago City Cemetery.

The area was quiet until 1989, when developers building luxury housing on the property got a nasty surprise. A backhoe operator dug up a corpse with his handlebar mustache still intact. The state had somehow lost track of the thousands of human remains underneath the land they sold to the developer. According to David Keene, the archaeologist on-site, "The area was just littered with human remains, with human bone all over the place, where they had disturbed things."

Today, Read Dunning Memorial Park stands as a tribute to the unknown people who lived and died at Dunning. The small memorial is in an open field surrounded by shopping centers and condos. Still, visitors take solace in the peaceful space, most without knowing what's underfoot.

86

MYSTERIOUS SANCTUARY

What's behind this mysterious church facade in Pilsen?

Art is everywhere in the South Side neighborhood of Pilsen, especially where you least expect it. One area church no longer serves as a house of worship, yet it remains a powerful and unexpected statement.

Zion Evangelical Lutheran looks normal enough as you approach it. The brick building stretches from 19th Street to the top of its clock tower ninety feet above. However, empty lancet windows frame the sky where you expect to see stained glass. Walk around the side of the building and you'll see that the sturdy front wall is all that's left of the structure. It looks more like a stage prop than a place of worship.

Back when it was built in 1880, the church had all four walls and a congregation to fill it. The neighborhood's German residents eventually moved elsewhere, and the congregation abandoned the church in 1956. The building suffered a fire in 1979 and was almost entirely destroyed by a windstorm in 1998. Owner and Pilsen developer John

At the turn of the twentieth century, Chicago was the third-largest Czech city in the world after Prague and Vienna. One Bohemian resident opened a restaurant on present-day 18th Street called "At the City of Plzen" in honor of his homeland. Residents began calling the neighborhood "Pilsen."

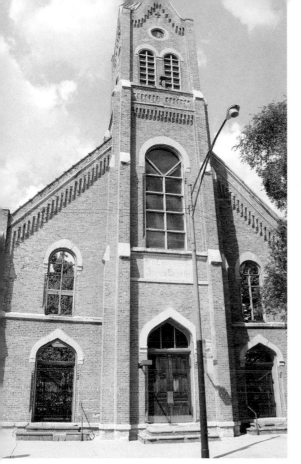

What appears to be a normal church is now a relic of the neighborhood's past that's been preserved.

ZION EVANGELICAL LUTHERAN

WHAT A church that's not what it seems

WHERE 19th and Peoria Sts.

COST Free

PRO TIP Access Pilsen's galleries and artist live/work spaces on the second Friday night of each month.

Podmajersky Jr. received a fateful visit the day after the storm. Descendants of the church's congregation delivered him an old book detailing the church's history in German.

"It was very moving," Podmajersky told the *Tribune* in 2000. "And it was that day I committed to save the tower no matter what." Podmajersky restored the church's tower and facade and added a skylight in place of the tower's roof. He planned to add artist studios to the site, but the plot is still vacant save some pieces of foundation. They stand in the lawn Podmajersky planted as an eerie sort of sculptural garden.

Many locals refer to the site as "The Sanctuary." What might have been the burnt shell of a building has been preserved as a symbol of the neighborhood's past and a surprising installation for those who pass by.

87 WEIRD SCIENCE

Where can I buy a spud launcher and a Wimshurst generator?

If you want to lose hours among the odd and obscure, a visit to American Science & Surplus is in order. Whether you're a tinkerer, crafter, or thingamajig enthusiast, the Northwest Side store's crammed aisles will spark your curiosity.

The store's offbeat offerings specialize in scientific and educational items and are organized into categories like lab equipment, militaria, and "robot partz." Looking for a silicone ballistic brain or Belgian ammo pouch? Look no further. As their website states, "We are fascinated by discovery and invention . . . and are dedicated to having fun along the way."

Chicagoan Al Luebbers founded American Science & Surplus in 1937. When he noticed a company throwing away rejected lenses, he hauled them off and began selling them. After World War II, the business expanded to include military surplus. The store eventually opened locations in Geneva, Illinois, and Milwaukee, Wisconsin. In 2012, the business was purchased by Patrick Meyer, a twenty-nine-year veteran of American Science & Surplus. Meyer worked

---

Even American Science & Surplus's bimonthly catalog is worth a read. The sixty-four-page newsprint guide lists more than 1,200 items, with amusing descriptions and illustrated drawings of each of them.

Part of the store's appeal is the handmade signs created for each item. Employees show off their uncommon sense of humor packed with pop culture references. The signs describe as much as American Science & Surplus knows about the item's origin.

AMERICAN SCIENCE & SURPLUS

WHAT Scientific surprises

WHERE 5316 N. Milwaukee Ave.

COST The cheapest items for sale start at five cents, and "high end" luxury items like telescopes can be yours for $99.99.

PRO TIP Overwhelmed? Purchase a mystery box of twenty-five dollars in odd or leftover merchandise for ten dollars. You can choose a surprise box of "electro-mechanical" items or a "consumer" box.

his way up from sweeping the store's floors to owning it!

Part of American Science & Surplus's draw is discovering odd items and one-of-a-kind equipment at prices you can't resist. As a surplus store, it sources most inventory through closeouts, overruns, and mis-manufactures. Once these unique surplus items are sold, there's no way to restock. It's best to stock up on industrial motors and fake snake eggs while you can!

If you've ever had the urge to raid your science teacher's supply cabinet, you can't miss American Science & Surplus. Every visit provides a new surprise, like the world's smallest postal scale or rubber duck feet. Suspend your disbelief and enjoy this bizarre scientific scavenger hunt!

88

NO HORSE IN THIS RACE

Can I go turtle racing in Chicago?

For many Andersonville residents, Friday night is spent at the races. The contestants aren't horses or even cars, but slow, surefooted turtles.

Every Friday night since 1997, neighborhood bar Big Joe's has hosted turtle racing. Spectators pour in ahead of the 9 p.m. start time to start earning race tickets. With wood paneling and carpeted floors, Big Joe's feels like drinking in a cozy living room. Every drink you purchase earns you tickets that will be entered into a raffle to determine the turtle jockeys. Tickets are pulled before each of the evening's six races. If you're lucky enough to serve as a turtle jockey, you'll pick a numbered ball from a bucket to be assigned a turtle.

The reptilian athletes go by the names Lucky Dan, Chicks, Lola, Doozy, Swisher, and Jolanda. The turtles are well cared for and live in a luxurious habitat upstairs. They're introduced with great fanfare as they enter the ring, an eight-foot series of colored circles painted on top of the racing table. The games begin when the turtles are placed on the ring under a clear cover. Once the cover comes off, the race is on!

BIG JOE'S

WHAT Heroes in a half shell

WHERE 1818 W. Foster Ave.

COST Free to watch, but you'll need to purchase drinks to earn the chance of turtle jockeying.

PRO TIP Hang in there! The loser of each round gets a free consolation beer.

Left, *Turtle racing may not be the fastest competition in town, but it's just as exciting.* Right, *Big Joe's draws big crowds for turtle racing. Arrive early to stake out a seat near the track.*

Spurred on from the chants and cheers of the audience, the competitors inch from the center of the table out toward the outermost blue line to victory in anywhere from three to five minutes. The first reptile to reach the edge is declared the winner. In the last race of the night, all winning turtle jockeys compete to be entered into the yearly tournament of champions with a grand prize trip to Las Vegas. However, last place has its perks. The losing turtle jockey gets a free drink, so everyone's a winner!

Each turtle has a personality. For example, Jolanda has a reputation for coming in last. Maybe she heard that losers get a free drink?

89

GOING UP?

Where can I ride in one of Chicago's only manually operated elevators?

Some buildings are home to all manner of secrets. Located on Michigan Avenue in the heart of the Loop, the Fine Arts Building is such a place. If you're looking for lore in a building that has hosted Chicago's artists for more than a century, just buzz the elevator.

It may surprise you to hear a ring as you press the button, and even more so as a clanking sound moves from floor to floor toward you. The wooden doors slide open to reveal a person who is quite literally the keeper of the key—the elevator operator.

The Fine Arts Building is one of the last in the city with full-time operators. It was built in 1885 as a Studebaker carriage factory and showroom. Studebaker moved out in 1898 and converted the building to artist spaces, and it's served Chicago's musicians, dancers, sculptors, and illustrators ever since.

The operator closes the door with a bang and asks where you're heading. If you don't know which floor, he certainly does. The glass panels provide a glimpse of each floor as you ascend. You launch past the fourth floor, where one hallway opens on the sunny Venetian Court. Past the fifth floor, where cellos are still crafted by hand. Past the tenth floor, where Frank Lloyd Wright once had a studio down the hall from a series of Art Nouveau murals.

FINE ARTS BUILDING

WHAT A distinctive ride in an artistic enclave

WHERE 410 S. Michigan Ave.

COST Free

PRO TIP See a stained glass window designed by Frank Lloyd Wright at the end of the second-floor hallway.

196

It's rare to find a building in any city that still has full-time elevator operators. The Fine Arts Building has three elevators to maintain and five elevator operators.

The floors fly by—former homes of Lorado Taft's studio, the space where Margaret Anderson serialized *Ulysses* in *The Little Review*, and the office where Harriet Monroe founded *Poetry* magazine and first published T. S. Eliot, Ezra Pound, and Carl Sandburg. You finally step out on the tenth floor, where W. W. Denslow illustrated *The Wonderful Wizard of Oz* in his studio.

Passing through the building, you'll hear different music on each floor. Violin gives way to piano or a vocalist practicing arias. The building is still buzzing with creative energy—and elevator buttons.

In 2000, the lobby was named Durkin Hall after longtime elevator operator Tommy Durkin, to commemorate his fiftieth anniversary at the Fine Arts Building. A plaque in the lobby is dedicated to Durkin, who retired in 2010 after sixty years of manning the controls of elevator car No. 1.

90

FOR ART'S SAKE

How did sculpture help save a community?

You won't see the Oakland Museum of Contemporary Art listed in guidebooks next to the Art Institute or the Museum of Contemporary Art. Yet this small space had a big hand in reviving the North Kenwood/Oakland community.

The little-known museum sits on two lots on East 41st Place near Berkeley Avenue. The landscaped lawns are dotted with abstract wooden sculptures, the work of the late artist Milton Mizenberg.

The South Side neighborhood looked quite different in the 1990s. Mizenberg lived across the street from the lots, and he didn't like the view outside. Tired of the litter, abandoned cars, and loitering gangs, he began improving the neighborhood one artwork at a time. The self-taught sculptor took a chainsaw to tree trunks, filling vacant lots with art. The Oakland Museum of Contemporary Art was born.

When kids asked what he was doing with the chainsaw, Mizenberg replied, per the *Tribune*, "I'm giving this art to you. And it's your responsibility to take care of it." He added several more wooden artworks, and the city even supplied

---

Mizenberg's first bronze sculpture is located across the street from the museum in Williams-Davis Park. Restoration is dedicated to "the men and women who remained in the Oakland community during difficult times and worked hard to restore its former beauty."

Restoration is Mizenberg's first work in bronze.

OAKLAND MUSEUM OF CONTEMPORARY ART

WHAT A community gallery

WHERE S. Berkeley Ave. and E. 41st Pl.

COST Free

NOTEWORTHY The gardens are still maintained by neighbors.

poplar, oak, and ash tree stumps. No pieces in the outdoor sculpture garden have ever been defaced.

After brightening up his neighborhood with art, Mizenberg spent years battling multiple myeloma. His neighbors kept him inspired by commissioning an artwork. Working through his life-threatening health problems, he created his first bronze sculpture.

Two decades later, Mizenberg's work lives on as a reminder of the power of hope, creativity, and community. As he told *Chicago Revealed* in 2010, "If you want to make a change in anything, you've got to do it. You can't just be speaking of it all the time. And that's what I did. I said 'I can do something on my block. I don't know how, but on my block I can.'"

APPENDIX

SOURCES

1. Presidential Kiss and Tell
http://www.oprah.com/world/Barack-and-Michelle-Obamas-First-Date-Famous-Firsts
http://articles.chicagotribune.com/2012-08-16/news/ct-talk-obama-kiss-marker-20120816_1_baskin-robbins-ice-cream-shop-historical-marker
https://www.nytimes.com/2017/01/09/us/politics/chicago-south-side-obama-farewell.html?_r=0
http://www.nbcchicago.com/news/local/Plaque-Marks-First-Couples-First-Kiss-Chicago-166393916.html

2. The Other Sears Tower
http://www.homansquare.org/history/sears-roebuck-and-co/
Sinkevitch, Alice, et al. *AIA Guide to Chicago*. University of Illinois Press, 2014.
http://openhousechicago.org/sites/site/nichols-tower-at-homan-square-original-sears-tower/
http://chicagotonight.wttw.com/2015/11/17/chicagos-original-sears-tower-reborn-community-center
http://www.willistower.com/history-and-facts

3. Creative Convenience
Miller, Dan. *At Work with Thomas Kong*, 2017.
http://mileofmurals.com/news.html
https://www.dnainfo.com/chicago/20170831/rogers-park/2-new-art-pieces-joining-mile-of-murals-rogers-park-this-fall
https://www.chicagoreader.com/chicago/loyola-beach-sea-bench-artists-of-the-wall-festival-loyola-park-advisory-council/Content?oid=14559601
https://rpba.org/2017/06/glenwood-sculpture-garden/

4. Knockin' on Heaven's Door
Tour on September 24, 2017.
http://www.chicagotemple.org/about
http://archives.chicagotribune.com/1981/06/27/page/10/article/church-will-mark-150th-year-here#text
http://abc7chicago.com/archive/9518865/

5. Flying High
Interview with Shayna Swanson, September 18, 2017.
http://www.aloftloft.com/
https://www.dnainfo.com/chicago/20161215/logan-square/aloft-circus-arts-logan-square-church-kimball-and-wrightwood-avenues
https://www.dnainfo.com/chicago/20160810/logan-square/logan-square-churchs-transformation-elite-circus-school-nearly-complete
http://www.chicagotribune.com/business/ct-chicago-circus-gyms-0319-biz-20170317-story.html

6. Rest in Pieces
http://articles.chicagotribune.com/1999-05-31/features/9905310107_1_von-grave-site-lake-michigan
https://www.dnainfo.com/chicago/20160609/east-side/this-tiny-secret-gravesite-features-soldier-who-fought-napoleon
https://www.dnainfo.com/chicago/20160620/portage-park/great-great-grandson-still-has-piece-of-tiny-secret-chicago-gravesite

7. Good Vibrations
Interview with Peter Mars, August 24, 2017.
McNeil, Brett. "A Brief History of Harmoniousness." *Chicago Journal*, May 23, 2002.
http://www.marsgallery.com/about.html
http://gapersblock.com/detour/uncovering_the_fulton_street_vortex/
https://www.chicagoarchitecture.org/2014/10/31/a-true-halloween-tale-if-your-creativity-is-waning-head-to-the-fulton-vortex/

8. Covert Cocktails
Interview with Luke Nevin-Gattle, August 17, 2017.
http://www.oldchicagoinn.com/rooms/room13.shtml
https://www.forbes.com/sites/megykarydes/2015/08/17/speakeasies-worth-the-visit/#54f9422f3683

9. Warriors without Weapons
http://infoweb.newsbank.com/resources/doc/nb/news/0EB37362D33E53CF?p=NewsBank
http://www.encyclopedia.chicagohistory.org/pages/80.html
http://chicagopublicart.blogspot.com/2013/08/the-bowman-and-spearman.html
http://www.choosechicago.com/articles/view/art-and-sculptures-in-grant-park-chicago/311/
https://cdn.citl.illinois.edu/courses/aiiopcmpss/essays/chicagomem/chicagomem10.htm
http://www.croatia.org/crown/articles/9922/1/Ivan-Mestrovic-Croatian-sculptor-and-his-Chicago-Indians.html#_ftnref15
https://www.timeout.com/chicago/things-to-do/warrior-statues-missing-weapons
http://articles.chicagotribune.com/2008-08-24/news/0808220701_1_public-art-picasso-art-deco

10. Dusty Hunting
http://infoweb.newsbank.com.gatekeeper.chipublib.org/resources/doc/nb/news/13D4019DDFB9EAF0?p=NewsBank
http://articles.chicagotribune.com/2009-01-22/news/0901200397_1_vinyl-soul-titles-record-store
http://adventures-of-darrell-d.blogspot.com/2016/07/vinyl-shop-spotlight-out-of-past-records.html
http://austintalks.org/2010/07/hours-speed-by-at-out-of-the-past-records/

11. Green Machine
Tour on July 8, 2017.
http://plantchicago.org/
http://www.huffingtonpost.com/2012/05/07/the-plant-explained-chicago-urban-farm_n_1497832.html
https://energy.gov/eere/energybasics/articles/anaerobic-digestion-basics
https://www.nrdc.org/onearth/former-meatpacking-facility-now-experiment-sustainable-urban-ag

12. That Toddlin' Town
https://www.cityofchicago.org/content/dam/city/depts/zlup/Historic_Preservation/Publications/Five_Brewery_Tied_Houses_and_One_Brewery_Stable.pdf
http://www.abdi.org
http://forgottenchicago.com/features/tied-houses/
http://articles.chicagotribune.com/2009-09-20/features/0909170447_1_pins-bowlers-show-bowling-alley

13. Button Up
Interview with Christen and Joel Carter, July 6, 2017.
https://www.busybeaver.net/
https://www.dnainfo.com/chicago/20150206/logan-square/worlds-only-button-museum-based-logan-square-plans-expansion
http://content.time.com/time/photogallery/0,29307,2106314,00.html

14. 'Til the Cows Come Home
https://chicagohistorytoday.wordpress.com/2015/08/17/the-cow-path-in-the-chicago-loop/
Taylor, Troy, et al. *Weird Chicago: Forgotten History, Strange Legends & Mysterious Hauntings of the Windy City.* Whitechapel Press, 2009.
http://chicagotonight.wttw.com/2011/08/17/hidden-chicago-streets-alleys
http://archives.chicagotribune.com/1979/03/29/page/127/article/loop-cow-path-for-big-moovers#text

15. It's a Highway to Heaven
Email: Janet Harper——CBMR Reference, Instruction & Community Engagement Librarian
http://www.chicagotribune.com/lifestyles/chi-bo-diddley-story.html
https://www.cityofchicago.org/content/dam/city/depts/zlup/Historic_Preservation/Publications/Ebenezer_Missionary_Baptist_Church.pdf
http://www.chicagotribune.com/news/nationworld/politics/chi-chicagodays-gospelmusic-story-story.html
https://webapps.cityofchicago.org/landmarksweb/web/landmarkdetails.htm?lanId=13328
http://archives.chicagotribune.com/1978/01/22/page/212/article/the-good-news-of-gospel#text
http://archives.chicagotribune.com/1980/02/09/page/50/article/the-father-of-gospel-music

16. Eye to the Sky
http://articles.chicagotribune.com/2006-05-11/features/0605100337_1_skyspace-public-art-james-turrell
http://www.newswise.com/articles/skyspace-opens-to-public-on-south-campus
http://archive.news.uic.edu/releases-2002-2012/1291-uic-dedicates-earl-l-neal-plaza-on-south-campus.html
Ford, Anne. *Peaceful Places, Chicago: 110 Tranquil Sites in the Windy City and Beyond.* Menasha Ridge Press, 2011.
Borzo, Greg, et al. *Chicago's Fabulous Fountains.* Southern Illinois University Press, 2017.

http://jamesturrell.com/about/introduction/
http://encyclopedia.chicagohistory.org/pages/794.html

17. Forgotten Terminal 4
https://www.wbez.org/shows/curious-city/ohares-ghost-whatever-happened-to-terminal-4/b06fdf34-c604-4391-a31e-600deea7ca4b
http://www.panynj.gov/airports/pdf-traffic/ATR2016.pdf
http://abcnews.go.com/Travel/history-airport-codes-logic-letter-codes/story?id=11684406
http://www.flychicago.com/ohare/en/aboutus/pages/history.aspx

18. Going Nuclear
http://fpdcc.com/site-a/
https://www.chicagoreader.com/chicago/here-lies-the-worlds-first-nuke/Content?oid=870570
https://www.chicagomaroon.com/2009/03/05/the-way-things-work-nuclear-waste/

19. Cairo Calling
http://archives.chicagotribune.com/1961/03/16/page/83/article/chicago-firm-keeps-egypt-in-warehouse#text
Taylor, Troy, et al. *Weird Illinois: Your Travel Guide to Illinois' Local Legends and Best Kept Secrets.* Sterling, 2012.
http://www.reebieallied.com/about-us/

20. A Home Run Logo
Interview with Patrick Hatton and Natalie Edwards, August 25, 2017.
http://www.chicagobusiness.com/article/20150601/BLOGS03/150539999/for-this-pritzker-chicago-athletic-association-hotel-redo-was-a-labor-of-love
http://www.chicagoathletichotel.com/michigan-avenue-hotel-blog/caa-cubs-a-place-in-history
http://www.chicagotribune.com/sports/baseball/cubs/ct-cubs-uniform-visual-history-htmlstory.html
http://www.sportslogos.net/logos/list_by_team/54/Chicago_Cubs/

21. A Room of One's Own
http://www.art.org/henry-darger-room-collection
http://www.officialhenrydarger.com/about/
http://www.chicagotribune.com/entertainment/museums/ct-henry-darger-intuit-gallery-ent-0316-20170315-column.html

22. Secret Garden
Interview with Jesse Zavala, September 12, 2017.
http://mbtchicago.org/about-the-temple/
http://chicagoshimpo.com/e-community/0808_lagacygarden_mbt.htm
https://www.dnainfo.com/chicago/20140811/old-town/photos-video-celebrating-japanese-culture-at-ginza-festival

23. Subterranean City
https://www.cityofchicago.org/city/en/depts/cdot/provdrs/ped/svcs/pedway.html
Chicago Elevated tour with Margaret Hicks, February 25, 2017.
http://www.chicagotribune.com/news/columnists/ct-pedway-architecture-kamin-met-1227-20161223-column.html
http://archives.chicagotribune.com/1989/12/14/page/81/article/at-long-last-tunnel-walkway-debuts

24. Art of House
https://rebuild-foundation.org/site/stony-island-arts-bank
http://www.chicagoreader.com/chicago/stony-island-arts-bank-frankie-knuckles-record-collection/Content?oid=19201984
http://www.chicagotribune.com/business/ct-harris-theater-gates-arts-bank-0906-biz-20150904-column.html
http://www.factmag.com/2015/09/23/frankie-knuckles-record-collection-chicago-stony-island-arts-bank/
https://www.theguardian.com/music/2014/apr/01/frankie-knuckles

25. No Bones about It
https://www.timeout.com/chicago/things-to-do/woolly-mammoth-antiques-oddities-resale
http://chicago.cbslocal.com/2017/01/16/made-in-chicago-woolly-mammoth/
http://www.columbiachronicle.com/arts_and_culture/article_fd9c2a9a-8aea-11e3-83be-001a4bcf6878.html

26. Excrement as Art
https://www.timeout.com/chicago/things-to-do/fountain-of-waste
http://www.chicagoreader.com/chicago/jerzy-kenar-shit-fountain-sculpture-east-village/
Content?oid=14316826

27. Circus Catastrophe
Taylor, Troy, et al. *Weird Chicago: Forgotten History, Strange Legends & Mysterious Hauntings of the Windy City.*
Whitechapel Press, 2009.
Morris, Jeff, and Vince Sheilds. *Chicago Haunted Handbook: 99 Ghostly Places You Can Visit in and around the
Windy City.* Clerisy Press, 2013.
http://archives.chicagotribune.com/1918/06/23/page/1/article/arrest-wreck-engineer#text
http://archives.chicagotribune.com/1983/07/15/page/394/article/woodlawn-cemetery#text
http://www.chicagotribune.com/news/opinion/commentary/ct-circus-train-showmens-rest-flashback-
perspec-0814-jm-20160810-story.html
http://www.showmensleague.org/Showmens-Rest

28. Hollywood Moment
https://www.timeout.com/chicago/things-to-do/albany-park-irving-park-secrets?package_page=21387
http://seligpolyscope.com/about/studio-history/
http://www.chicagomag.com/Chicago-Magazine/May-2007/Reel-Chicago/
http://www.chicagotribune.com/news/nationworld/politics/chi-chicagodays-essanaystudios-story-story.
html
http://mysteriouschicago.com/podcast-selig-polyscope-studios/
http://www.lakeviewhistoricalchronicles.org/2012/02/holly-view-film-studios.html

29. Buzzing Along
http://www.wildblossommeadery.com/What-is-Mead
https://www.chicagoreader.com/Bleader/archives/2017/02/21/illinoiss-only-true-meadery-is-riding-the-
current-wave-of-interest-in-the-fermented-honey-beverage
http://mead-makers.org/about-mead/

30. An Explosive Lawn Ornament
http://www.wickerparkbucktown.info/content-arts/wicker-parks-historic-mansions-beer-baron-row
https://webapps.cityofchicago.org/landmarksweb/web/districtdetails.htm?disId=36
http://www.chicagoreader.com/chicago/wicker-park-american-legion-cannon/Content?oid=7482339
https://www.dnainfo.com/chicago/20161122/wicker-park/howitzer-cannon-wicker-park-hoyne-avenue

31. Saved from the Wrecking Ball
Vinci, John, and Pauline A. Saliga. *The Trading Room: Louis Sullivan and the Chicago Stock Exchange.* Art Institute
of Chicago, 1989.
http://www.artic.edu/about/event-planning/event-spaces/chicago-stock-exchange-trading-room
http://archives.chicagotribune.com/1980/08/17/page/296/article/article-4-no-title#text
http://archives.chicagotribune.com/1960/04/24/page/270/article/closeup-view-of-stock-exchange-floor-
intense-exciting-vital
http://archives.chicagotribune.com/1984/06/01/page/148/article/weekend-guide#text

32. As Seen on TV
http://openhousechicago.org/sites/site/zap-props/
http://chicagotonight.wttw.com/2016/03/29/look-inside-chicagos-largest-prop-house
http://halfstackmagazine.blogspot.com/2014/09/halfstack-fall-issue-sneak-peek-zap.html
https://www.dnainfo.com/chicago/20160620/bridgeport/zap-props-bridgeport-has-just-about-every-
item-you-can-imagine-really

33. The Leaning Tower of Niles
https://www.vniles.com/883/The-Leaning-Tower-of-Niles
http://articles.chicagotribune.com/2013-09-10/news/ct-tl-niles-leaning-tower-renovation-20130830_1_
tower-tilt-niles-trustees-vinezeano
http://archives.chicagotribune.com/1953/07/05/page/123/article/leaning-tower-still-startles-niles-
visitors
http://www.journal-topics.com/news/article_609f26c8-f3cb-11e6-ba7f-3f42337ba57d.html- legal
http://buglenewspapers.com/niles-mayor-looks-to-improve-government-attract-businesses - legal

34. The Curious Couch Tomb
Taylor, Troy, et al. *Weird Chicago: Forgotten History, Strange Legends & Mysterious Hauntings of the Windy City.*
Whitechapel Press, 2009.

Selzer, Adam. *Mysterious Chicago: History at Its Coolest.* Skyhorse Publishing, 2016.

http://gapersblock.com/airbags/archives/who_is_buried_in_couchs_tomb/

http://articles.chicagotribune.com/2008-05-21/news/0805200445_1_graveyard-archeologists-park-visitors

http://mysteriouschicago.com/whos-buried-in-ira-couchs-tomb-some-new-info/

http://articles.chicagotribune.com/1993-01-03/features/9303150301_1_crypt-city-park-chicago

http://hiddentruths.northwestern.edu/couch/stories.html

35. Sweet Tooth

http://www.encyclopedia.chicagohistory.org/pages/2463.html

http://www.blommer.com/the-difference-history.php

http://www.blommer.com/_documents/blommer-product-offerings-brochure.pdf

http://articles.chicagotribune.com/2014-05-18/business/ct-chocolate-smell-chicago-blommer-biz-0518-20140518_1_cocoa-henry-blommer-blommer-chocolate-co

http://www.chicagotribune.com/news/columnists/schmich/ct-smells-chicago-schmich-1008-20141008-column.html

https://www.dnainfo.com/chicago/20141006/west-loop/meet-man-behind-daily-chicago-chocolate-smell-map

https://www.thisamericanlife.org/radio-archives/episode/307/transcript

http://archives.chicagotribune.com/1980/01/02/page/3/article/success-is-sweet-in-candy-fire

http://www.chicagobusiness.com/article/20051103/NEWS07/200018388/blommer-pumping-too-much-chocolate-into-air-epa

http://articles.chicagotribune.com/2005-11-04/news/0511040117_1_opacity-violations-power-plants-cocoa-powder

36. The Hidden Gallery

Tour with Sidney Hamper, September 16, 2017.

http://www.encyclopedia.chicagohistory.org/pages/134.html

http://vanderpoelartmuseum.org/?page_id=31

http://articles.chicagotribune.com/1995-06-11/features/9506110377_1_paintings-artist-and-teacher-human-figure

https://www.dnainfo.com/chicago/20140529/beverly/priceless-vanderpoel-art-collection-tucked-within-beverlys-ridge-park

https://www.chicagoreader.com/chicago/separation-anxiety/Content?oid=912396

37. No-Fly Zone

https://www.wbez.org/shows/curious-city/zeppelin-poseurs-why-chicagos-airship-dreams-never-took-off/6bc1ecca-8e29-45c6-a8ed-1e5d58d38a3c

http://www.chicagocarless.com/2008/05/19/inside-the-onion-dome-atop-the-intercontinental-chicago-hotel/

http://www.historichotels.org/hotels-resorts/intercontinental-chicago-magnificent-mile/history.php

Bizzarri, Amy. *Discovering Vintage Chicago: A Guide to the City's Timeless Shops, Bars, Delis & More.* GPP, 2015.

https://www.icchicagohotel.com/explore/

http://d3nldp8os5lzfq.cloudfront.net/AIDAJDTO4ONEOVG2YBJQ4/cms/pressroom/history_pdf_152017.pdf

38. Ground Control

Interview with Jim Bachor, July 24, 2017.

http://www.bachor.com/4600-north-kenton---map

http://www.chicagomag.com/Chicago-Magazine/March-2017/Why-We-Love-Chicago/Pothole-Art/

http://www.chicagotribune.com/news/ct-pothole-artist-kickstarter-met-0227-20160229-story.html

http://articles.chicagotribune.com/2014-03-31/entertainment/ct-pothole-art-20140401_1_pothole-season-mosaic-marble

39. A Cut Above

https://imss.org/

http://archives.chicagotribune.com/1969/09/18/page/108/article/surgeons-hall-marks-15th-year/#text

http://archives.chicagotribune.com/1986/09/05/page/106/article/believe-it-or-not-museums-can-surprise#text

40. All Dolled Up

Interview with Jojo Baby, September 14, 2017.

http://www.huffingtonpost.com/entry/meet-jojo-baby-a-legend-in-the-chicago-worlds-of-queer-art-and-nightlife_us_5644b274e4b045bf3dedf499

http://oururbantimes.com/arts/meet-jojo-baby-person

http://5chicago.com/features/jojo-baby-interview/

https://www.rainbowed.us/pop-cult/in-profile-jojo-baby/
https://www.chicagoreader.com/chicago/clive-barker-jojo-baby/Content?oid=2660181

41. 'Til Death Do Us Part
http://www.chicagotribune.com/news/ct-chicago-tour-guides-recommend-graves-to-visit-20161031-htmlstory.html
http://www.orderofthegooddeath.com/the-italian-bride-of-chicago

42. Sleeping Giants
http://arcchicago.blogspot.com/2013/07/the-power-of-useless-history-and.html
http://americanurbex.com/wordpress/?p=839
https://www.bisnow.com/chicago/news/commercial-real-estate/inside-chicagos-most-mysterious-property-42350#0
https://newcity.com/grain-of-truth-taking-stock-of-the-relics-of-chicagos-era-as-the-worlds-stacker-of-wheat/
Ketchum, Milo Smith. *Design of Walls, Bins and Grain Elevators.* Nabu Press, 2010.
http://www.chicagoparkdistrict.com/parks/canalport-riverwalk-park/#k1vpuyxcel
https://www.scientificamerican.com/article/the-handling-and-storage-of-our-hug/
"New Grain Elevator for the Santa Fe System at Chicago." *The Railway Age*, March 23, 1906, pp. 408–410.
books.google.com/books?id=0Z9MAAAAYAAJ&pg=PA408&lpg=PA408&dq=new+grain+elevator+for+the+santa+fe+system+at+chicago&source=bl&ots=b_ke8ykcOX&sig=bSjazT-6LeTXbT9mZa8T0w05G_I&hl=en&sa=X&ved=0ahUKEwjV5sjB1uvSAhUh0IMKHdiUBzcQ6AEINDAE#v=onepage&q=new%20grain%20elevator%20for%20the%20santa%20fe%20system%20at%20chicago&f=false.

43. Worth One's Salt
http://www.galoscaves.com/_en/ofirmie.htm
http://articles.chicagotribune.com/2008-01-17/entertainment/0801150385_1_salt-rocks-salt-caves-crystal-salt
http://illawarrasalttherapy.com.au/history

44. The Original Blues Brothers
Tour with Janine Judge, September 27, 2017.
Richards, Keith, et al. *Life.* Bruna, 2010.
https://www.songhall.org/profile/willie_dixon
http://openvault.wgbh.org/catalog/V_0FDCCD5CA2EB47BAA80E9DDD21954D05
http://www.chicagotribune.com/entertainment/music/ct-musicians-who-recorded-with-chicago-s-chess-records-20161019-photogallery.html
http://chicago.suntimes.com/news/phil-chess-legendary-founder-of-chess-records-dies-at-95/
http://www.bluesheaven.com

45. The Wonderful Park of Oz
http://www.lincolncentral.org/oz-park/
Holden, Greg. *Literary Chicago: A Book Lover's Tour of the Windy City.* Lake Claremont Press, 2001.
Larson, Erik. *The Devil in the White City.* Vintage, 2004.
http://archives.chicagotribune.com/1976/08/12/page/18/article/blue-collar-views#text
http://www.chicagoparkdistrict.com/parks/Oz-Park/
http://articles.chicagotribune.com/1995-10-02/news/9510020140_1_tin-man-sculpture-yellow-brick-road

46. Secret Street
http://chi.streetsblog.org/2016/10/25/central-area-committee-pushing-new-downtown-rail-transit-again/
http://chicagoloopbridges.com/FAQS12.html#ans1-4b
http://1001chicago.com/541/
http://webapps.cityofchicago.org/landmarksweb/web/landmarkdetails.htm?lanId=13091&counter=53
http://archives.chicagotribune.com/1980/12/26/page/23/article/an-armchair-historians-street-guide-to-chicago#text
http://historicbridges.org/bridges/browser/?bridgebrowser=truss/nbrail/

47. Humongous Hot Dogs
http://www.chicagotribune.com/business/ct-hot-dog-emoji-1024-biz-20151023-story.html
Bizzarri, Amy. *Discovering Vintage Chicago: A Guide to the City's Timeless Shops, Bars, Delis & More.* GPP, 2015.
http://www.superdawg.com/history.cfm
http://www.chicagotribune.com/business/ct-hot-dog-emoji-1024-biz-20151023-story.html

48. Classified Supplies
Interview with Tyler Stoltenberg, September 26, 2017.

http://www.826chi.org/about/mission_facts/
https://www.secretagentsupply.com/

49. Dance-Floor Diplomacy
Interview with Gavin Rayna Russom, September 6, 2017.
Interview with Scott Cramer, July 11, 2017.
http://www.chicagotribune.com/redeye-berlin-owners-celebrate-30-years-as-chicagos-best-nongay-gay-club-20131104-story.html
http://www.berlinchicago.com/about.html

50. Chicago Craftsmanship
Tour with Zac Bleicher, August 9, 2017.
Cahan, Richard, et al. *Edgar Miller and the Handmade Home: Chicago's Forgotten Renaissance Man.* CityFiles Press, 2009.
http://www.edgarmiller.org/about/
https://www.chicagoreader.com/chicago/always-an-artist/Content?oid=881817
http://www.chicagomodern.org/artists/edgar_miller/

51. Alphabet Town
http://www.chsmedia.org/househistory/namechanges/start.pdf
http://www.chicagonow.com/north-by-northwest-side/2012/02/k-streets-conundrums-not-the-k-car-k-streets/
http://windycityguide.blogspot.com/2008/06/street-names-in-chicago-k-town-and-why.html
http://chicago.straightdope.com/sdc20100121.php

52. Rock On
Kamin, Blair, and Bob Fila. *Tribune Tower, American Landmark: History, Architecture, and Design.* Tribune Co., 2000.
http://www.chicagotribune.com/news/columnists/ct-ballpark-bricks-kamin-met-0814-20150813-column.html
http://archives.chicagotribune.com/1922/12/03/page/1/article/howells-wins-in-contest-for-tribune-tower

53. Sugar High
http://dulcelandia.com/index.php
https://www.dnainfo.com/chicago/20160930/little-village/frozen-yogurt-dulcelandia-yogolandia-mexican-flavors
https://www.chicagoreader.com/chicago/dulcelandia-pinata-hermosa-mexico-candy-eduardo-rodriguez/Content?oid=12001015
http://www.chicagobusiness.com/section/little-village
https://www.chicagoreader.com/chicago/26th-street-little-village-shopping-corridor/BestOf?oid=27092360
http://chicago.cbslocal.com/2015/10/14/little-village-retail-strip-is-second-highest-grossing-in-city/
https://www.cnbc.com/2017/05/02/how-successful-immigrant-entrepreneurs-are-changing-chicago-and-the-us.html

54. A League of Their Own
http://www.nbcchicago.com/news/local/cubs-mausoleum-bohemian-national-cemetery-chicago-burial-397157641.html
http://www.bleedcubbieblue.com/2013/10/31/5044566/the-sordid-travels-of-a-cubs-fan-the-afterlife
http://wgntv.com/2016/11/01/cubs-inspired-cemetery-is-a-friendly-confines-for-the-afterlife/
http://www.eastlanddisaster.org/news/BNC-dedicates-memorial-to-eastland-victims
http://articles.chicagotribune.com/2009-08-12/news/0908110640_1_cubs-logo-dennis-mascari-white-sox-fan
http://www.chicagotribune.com/news/ct-eastland-disaster-memorial-met-20150712-story.html
http://www.espn.com/mlb/news/story?id=3484045

55. Jugheads
http://www.tobyjugmuseum.com/
http://abc7chicago.com/archive/6535034/

56. Underground Chinatown
http://fooditor.com/fooditor-guide-chinatowns-richland-food-court-2017-edition/
https://www.chicagoreader.com/Bleader/archives/2010/10/28/going-down-at-richland-center-chinatown
http://encyclopedia.chicagohistory.org/pages/284.html

http://articles.chicagotribune.com/2004-03-07/news/0403070531_1_tse-tung-mao-china

57. Lights, Camera, Action!
Interview with Gordon Quinn, September 28, 2017.
Harris, Scott Jordan. *World Film Locations Chicago.* Intellect Books, 2013.
https://www.kartemquin.com/about/history
http://www.chicagotribune.com/entertainment/movies/ct-chicago-kartemquin-50th-anniversary-documentaries-20151203-column.html
http://www.rogerebert.com/interviews/documentary-buddha-gordon-quinn-on-the-legacy-of-kartemquin-films
http://infoweb.newsbank.com.gatekeeper.chipublib.org/resources/doc/nb/news/0F4F52FBA802D513?p=NewsBank

58. The Drifter
Interview with Allison Dincecco, August 17, 2017.
http://www.greendoorchicago.com/history
http://chicago.suntimes.com/entertainment/diners-notebook-the-drifter-speakeasy-to-open-underneath-green-door-tavern/
http://www.chibarproject.com/Reviews/GreenDoor/GreenDoor.htm

59. The Most Beautiful Church in America
http://www.cantius.org/go/about_us/
http://www.chicagotribune.com/news/local/breaking/ct-st-cantius-church-award-met-2-20160419-story.html
McNamara, Denis R., and James Morris. *Heavenly City: The Architectural Tradition of Catholic Chicago.* Liturgy Training Publications, 2005.

60. Follow the Wooden Block Road
https://search-proquest-com.gatekeeper.chipublib.org/hnpchicagotribune/docview/168706092/F6138A5737124FD4PQ/1?accountid=303
Eleventh Annual Report of the Board of Public Works to the Common Council. 1872.
http://arcchicago.blogspot.com/2011/10/how-bunch-of-blockheads-restored.html
https://www.dnainfo.com/chicago/20160526/auburn-gresham/many-of-chicagos-wooden-streets-are-still-intact-thyere-just-paved-over

61. Big Shoes to Fill
The Chicago Public Art Guide. The Department of Cultural Affairs and Special Events, www.cityofchicago.org/content/dam/city/depts/dca/Public%20Art/publicartguide1.pdf.
http://articles.chicagotribune.com/2006-11-17/news/0611170409_1_magdalena-abakanowicz-sculptures-headless
http://articles.chicagotribune.com/2006-10-27/news/0610270183_1_magdalena-abakanowicz-sculptures-headless
http://www.abakanowicz.art.pl/
http://infoweb.newsbank.com.gatekeeper.chipublib.org/resources/doc/nb/news/115079A434A8CA08?p=NewsBank

62. On Your Mark
http://www.nwitimes.com/business/local/historic-marktown-almost-but-future-uncertain/article_11b906f8-7332-574a-bea7-a91e0995ce60.html
http://www.marktown.org/tour.html
http://www.chicagotribune.com/news/ct-met-marktown-20130418-story.html
http://news.medill.northwestern.edu/chicago/happy-anniversary-marktown-100th-year-surviving/
https://www.choosechicago.com/blog/post/explore-chicagos-historic-alta-vista-terrace-district/

63. Otherworldly Reads
Interview with Louvel Delon, September 28, 2017.
http://www.occultbookstore.com/who-we-are/
http://bookstoresofchicago.tumblr.com/post/52241168765/the-occult-bookstore
https://www.groupon.com/articles/i-went-to-meet-my-spirit-guide-at-wicker-parks-occult-bookstore-and-found-a-unicorn-instead-al
http://www.nwitimes.com/entertainment/columnists/offbeat/offbeat-chicago-occult-bookstore-and-its--plus-year-history/article_49b84dd0-53ea-5317-abf7-6e588461b6f4.html

64. The Life Aquatic
http://www.museum.mtu.edu/sites/default/files/AESMM_Web_Pub_1_Great_Lakes_Geology_0.pdf
https://www.chicagomaroon.com/2013/02/21/sunken-treasure-a-ship-and-a-shoal-off-49th-street/

http://chicagotonight.wttw.com/2012/09/26/shipwreck-chicagos-shore-line
http://chicagoist.com/2013/05/20/chicago_shipwreck_hiding_in_plain_s.php#photo-1
http://archives.chicagotribune.com/1899/09/26/page/1/article/alleged-theft-of-a-steamer#text
http://www.chicagotribune.com/news/photo/souffle/ct-beneath-the-surface-at-morgan-shoal-20160803-story.html
http://archives.chicagotribune.com/1914/07/19/page/8/article/silver-spray-breaks-up
http://digital.chipublib.org/cdm/compoundobject/collection/examiner/id/62375/rec/1
Chicago Examiner, Vol. 12, no. 177

65. Proud Performance

http://nativenewsonline.net/currents/end-era-american-indian-center-chicago-moves-wilson-avenue-location/
http://www.chicagotribune.com/news/ct-american-indian-center-powow-met-20161126-story.html
http://www.mitchellmuseum.org/
http://www.crazycrow.com/site/event/american-indian-center-chicago-powwow/
https://www.aicchicago.org/

66. Hidden Oasis

http://www.encyclopedia.chicagohistory.org/pages/669.html
http://www.seriouseats.com/2008/10/fine-falafel-oasis-cafe-chicago-loop-illinois.html

67. Capture the Flag

http://articles.chicagotribune.com/1985-04-25/sports/8501250228_1_decorations-oldest-flag-queen-elizabeth
http://www.wgnflag.com
http://voyagechicago.com/interview/meet-carl-gus-porter-iii-wgn-flag-decorating-co-south-side-8th-ward/
http://wgntv.com/2016/06/14/wgn-flag-co-no-relation-part-of-fabric-of-the-citys-history/

68. Get on Your Soapbox

Taylor, Troy, et al. *Weird Chicago: Forgotten History, Strange Legends & Mysterious Hauntings of the Windy City.* Whitechapel Press, 2009.
http://archives.chicagotribune.com/1971/06/24/page/155/article/ghosts-fill-the-air-as-bughouse-square-of-old-dies#text
http://archives.chicagotribune.com/1988/02/14/page/320/article/history#text
http://archives.chicagotribune.com/1956/02/26/page/117/article/impressions-of-chicago-in-the-hobohemia-of-old#text
http://archives.chicagotribune.com/1958/11/23/page/223/article/chicagos-new-left-bank#text
http://archives.chicagotribune.com/1989/09/24/page/49/article/bughouse-boxers-square-off-verbally#text
http://archives.chicagotribune.com/1987/07/20/page/1/article/bughouse-square-debates-become-the-rage-again-for-a-day#text
http://www.chicagotribune.com/entertainment/ct-newberry-bughouse-square-ent-0718-20170717-column.html

69. On the Right Track

http://thesilverpalmrestaurant.com/History.html
https://www.dnainfo.com/chicago/20140429/river-west/silver-palm-americas-greatest-sandwich-make-triumphant-return
http://www.npr.org/sections/waitwait/2011/03/25/134733849/sandwich-monday-the-three-little-piggy-sandwich
http://infoweb.newsbank.com.gatekeeper.chipublib.org/resources/doc/nb/news/0F0851DA1813676A?p=NewsBank
http://infoweb.newsbank.com.gatekeeper.chipublib.org/resources/doc/nb/news/0F82B202D75CEA43?p=NewsBank
http://www.davehoekstra.com/2020/03/02/bouquet-for-a-bar-the-matchbox-is-sold, Interview with Gregg Weinstein on 3/8/21

70. Smile Like You Mean It

http://www.nwitimes.com/uncategorized/calumet-city-centennial-cal-city-puts-on-a-happy-face/article_08c11219-f90a-5cf5-8bcf-4be8462a681d.html
Taylor, Troy, et al. *Weird Illinois: Your Travel Guide to Illinois' Local Legends and Best Kept Secrets.* Sterling, 2012.
http://www.calumetcitychamber.com/slide-view/about/

71. Secret Civil War

https://www.wbez.org/shows/curious-city/chicagos-forgotten-civil-war-prison-camp/2aea8281-878c-436f-8311-62747b7be31f

http://www.chicagotribune.com/entertainment/ct-camp-douglas-bell-a-grim-part-of-chicago-history-20150421-column.html

http://articles.chicagotribune.com/2013-05-31/entertainment/ct-ae-0602-kogan-sidewalks-20130531_1_ghosts-civil-war-stephen-a

https://www.dnainfo.com/chicago/20160524/douglas/south-side-civil-war-prison-camp-turning-up-bones-buttons

72. Wait a Minute, Mr. Postman

http://www.connectingthewindycity.com/2012/12/steve-goodman-post-office.html

http://www.wpamurals.com/lakeview.htm

http://www.compassrose.org/uptown/Uptown-Post-Office.html

http://www.uptownupdate.com/2010/06/culture-corner-uptown-post-office.html

https://livingnewdeal.org/projects/logan-square-station-post-office-sculpture-chicago-il/

http://interactive.wttw.com/a/chicago-stories-mural-preservation-project

73. Too Close for Comfort

https://www.goodmantheatre.org/About/

http://www.newyorker.com/magazine/2006/10/09/skulduggery

https://www.chicagoreader.com/chicago/as-del-lay-dying/Content?oid=1109931

http://www.orderofthegooddeath.com/wanna-see-a-famous-skull

http://www.playbill.com/article/chicagos-goodman-theatre-gets-a-head-via-late-actor-del-close-com-82919

74. Fit to Be Tied

https://www.leatherarchives.org/about_.html

http://infoweb.newsbank.com.gatekeeper.chipublib.org/resources/doc/nb/news/1375D9EE6DCF8618?p=NewsBank

http://articles.chicagotribune.com/2004-04-12/news/0404130001_1_leather-lovers-whips-memorial-day-weekend

http://articles.chicagotribune.com/2000-02-18/features/0002180012_1_museum-s-executive-director-new-site-leather-outfit

75. Tiny Town

http://www.thevillachicago.com/aboutthevilla/foundingofthevilla.html

https://chicago.curbed.com/2015/2/24/9988278/getting-to-know-chicagos-smallest-neighborhood-the-villa

http://francesarcher.com/2010/06/chicago-not-so-hidden-gem/

http://infoweb.newsbank.com.gatekeeper.chipublib.org/resources/doc/nb/news/0EB4214C35141526?p=NewsBank

https://webapps.cityofchicago.org/landmarksweb/web/districtdetails.htm?disId=31

76. Field of Dreams

http://search.proquest.com.gatekeeper.chipublib.org/chicagotribune/docview/291148396/FA54867B25BD4B16PQ/57?accountid=303

http://archives.iit.edu/technews/volume140/tnvol140no9.pdf

http://mypages.iit.edu/~johnsonpo/baseball.html

http://articles.chicagotribune.com/1991-08-31/sports/9103050358_1_pony-league-jack-brickhouse-comiskey-park

http://articles.chicagotribune.com/1990-08-28/news/9003120381_1_iwo-jima-farm-systems-rhode-island-college

http://infoweb.newsbank.com.gatekeeper.chipublib.org/resources/doc/nb/news/0EB421A39616D09C?p=NewsBank

http://infoweb.newsbank.com.gatekeeper.chipublib.org/resources/doc/nb/news/0EB421855F6D9EB2?p=NewsBank

http://chicagotonight.wttw.com/2016/10/05/ask-geoffrey-league-chicago-s-own

77. Walk the Line

https://rpwrhs.org/portfolio/the-indian-boundary-line/

https://www.choosechicago.com/neighborhoods/north/rogers-park/

https://www.chicagoreader.com/chicago/rogers-park-west-ridge-history/Content?oid=1483752

http://www.chicagoparkdistrict.com/parks/indian-boundary-park/

78. On the Move

Taylor, Troy, et al. *Weird Illinois: Your Travel Guide to Illinois' Local Legends and Best Kept Secrets.* Sterling, 2012.

http://mysteriouschicago.com/inez-clarke-the-ghost-a-girl-thats-never-been/

http://www.strangerdimensions.com/2013/08/10/inez-clarke-the-haunted-statue-of-graceland-cemetery/
http://www.cemeteryguide.com/inezclarke.html
http://infoweb.newsbank.com.gatekeeper.chipublib.org/resources/doc/nb/news/12BABD6E172DEDF0?p=NewsBank

79. Close Encounters of the Chicago Kind
Taylor, Troy, et al. *Weird Illinois: Your Travel Guide to Illinois' Local Legends and Best Kept Secrets.* Sterling, 2012.
http://www.cufos.org/org.html
http://www.hollywoodreporter.com/live-feed/history-orders-ufo-drama-blue-book-robert-zemeckis-1007663
https://www.bleedingcool.com/2017/05/28/robert-zemeckis-history-channel-ufo-investigation-series-blue-book/
http://infoweb.newsbank.com.gatekeeper.chipublib.org/resources/doc/nb/news/1201683972A53D90?p=NewsBank
http://www.northbynorthwestern.com/story/the-center-for-ufo-studies-that-northwestern-wante/

80. The Last Pioneer
Taylor, Troy, et al. *Weird Chicago: Forgotten History, Strange Legends & Mysterious Hauntings of the Windy City.* Whitechapel Press, 2009.
http://archives.chicagotribune.com/1921/02/04/page/8/article/editorial-of-the-day
http://www.downesstudio.net/img_2010/lcjaprilstreeter.html
http://mysteriouschicago.com/the-curse-of-captain-streeter/

81. Fit for a King
Tour with Rocko Onan on 9/3/17
https://goldpyramid.com/about/
http://goldpyramid.com/wp-content/uploads/2016/11/A-point-of-interest.pdf
http://goldpyramid.com/wp-content/uploads/2016/11/Pyramid-House-reopens-to-public.pdf
http://articles.chicagotribune.com/1988-07-20/news/8801160286_1_great-pyramid-three-pyramid-scale-replica
https://www.enjoyillinois.com/explore/listing/gold-pyramid-house

82. Pipe Dreams
Interview with Richard Bley 9/24/17
Sinkevitch, Alice, et al. *AIA Guide to Chicago.* University of Illinois Press, 2014.
http://www.iwanries.com/about-us.cfm
http://www.cigaraficionado.com/webfeatures/show/id/15705
http://archives.chicagotribune.com/1976/12/19/page/273/article/the-old-pipes-of-man-play-to-collectors#text
http://archives.chicagotribune.com/1967/10/02/page/47/article/article-8-no-title#text

83. Eye Can See Clearly Now
http://chicagotonight.wttw.com/2013/10/16/ask-geoffrey-1016
Taylor, Troy, et al. *Weird Chicago: Forgotten History, Strange Legends & Mysterious Hauntings of the Windy City.* Whitechapel Press, 2009.
Headley, Kathleen J. *Legendary Locals of Chicago Lawn and West Lawn.* Legendary Locals, 2015.

84. All That Jazz
https://www.chicagoreader.com/chicago/uptown-greenmilljazz-bar-history-owner-bartender-musicians/Content?oid=12784766
http://www.uptownchicagocommission.org/jun_2_03.htm
http://www.washingtontimes.com/news/2007/may/10/20070510-115457-2674r/
http://www.chicagotribune.com/entertainment/museums/ct-chicago-tavern-history-series-08192015-column.html

85. Grave Mistake
Selzer, Adam. *The Ghosts of Chicago: The Windy City's Most Famous Haunts.* Llewellyn Publications, 2013.
Morris, Jeff, and Vince Sheilds. *Chicago Haunted Handbook: 99 Ghostly Places You Can Visit in and around the Windy City.* Clerisy Press, 2013.
http://archives.chicagotribune.com/1874/02/22/page/5/article/suffering-humanity#text
https://www.wbez.org/shows/curious-city/the-story-of-dunning-a-tomb-for-the-living/6d71dc74-bb21-4a25-8980-c2d7a5670b06
http://www.alchemyofbones.com/stories/dunning.htm
https://www.chicagoreader.com/chicago/grave-mistake/Content?oid=874451

https://www.dnainfo.com/chicago/20160628/dunning/oak-park-avenue-be-moved-avoid-long-forgotten-bodies

86. Mysterious Sanctuary

https://www.chicagoreader.com/chicago/pilsen-zion-evangelical-lutheran-church-empty-19th-peoria-podmajersky/Content?oid=14795977

http://articles.chicagotribune.com/2000-05-21/features/0005210365_1_church-tower-inspiration-walls

http://www.encyclopedia.chicagohistory.org/pages/2477.html

http://www.encyclopedia.chicagohistory.org/pages/153.html

87. Weird Science

https://www.sciplus.com/AboutUs

https://www.washingtonpost.com/graphics/lifestyle/vacation-ideas/things-to-do-in-milwaukee/

http://archive.jsonline.com/business/whimsy-sells-at-american-science--surplus-2d7rjlu-181462061.html/

https://www.chicagoreader.com/chicago/whole-lotta-everything/Content?oid=889942

88. No Horse in This Race

https://www.thrillist.com/drink/chicago/lincoln-square/the-do-s-and-don-ts-of-turtle-racing-at-big-joe-s

http://www.upchicago.com/turtle-racing-at-big-joes

89. Going Up?

http://archives.chicagotribune.com/1980/05/18/page/268/article/the-fine-arts-building-bounces-back#text

http://chicago.suntimes.com/news/fine-arts-building-story/

http://www.npr.org/2016/06/07/481058620/chicagos-fine-arts-building-has-10-floors-but-innumerable-stories

http://articles.chicagotribune.com/2013-03-13/news/ct-met-tommy-durkin-obit-20130313_1_elevator-online-tribute-sisters

90. For Art's Sake

https://www.youtube.com/watch?v=WvRFQBs3NcI

http://articles.chicagotribune.com/2006-02-05/features/0602050405_1_urban-pioneers-comeback-cities-paul-s-grogan/7

http://www.detourart.com/milton-mizenberg-and-his-oakland-museum-of-contemporary-art/

http://articles.chicagotribune.com/2003-08-03/news/0308030273_1_sculpture-garden-oakland-neighborhood-contemporary-art

INDEX